A TAX-FREE WORLD!!

A TAX-FREE WORLD!!
The New Macroeconomic Model Theory...

DIYER ANDRES PARRA MUÑOZ

All rights reserved © 2023 by Diyer Andres Parra M.

To my lovely wife, Angela, my two amazingly smart kids, Pablo and Angel, that they all make my life happy every day.

TABLE OF CONTENTS

INTRODUCTION 7
CHAPTER I 9
WHERE WE COME FROM AND WHERE WE ARE NOW. 9
   WHAT IS THE HISTORY ON TAXES, WHERE THEY COME FROM? 10
   THE ROLE OF TAXES IN MODERN SOCIETIES? 12
   USD CURRENCY HISTORY AND WORLD IMPACT. 15
   THE EURO AND ITS HISTORY. 18
CHAPTER II 28
MY MACROECONOMIC THEORY 28
   THE CONCEPT OF A TAX-FREE WORLD. 29
   WHY SOME COUNTRIES DON'T RELY ON TAXES AND WHICH ONES? 31
   NOTABLE MISUSES OF TAXPAYER FUNDS: 39
   TAX PAYERS AND THE WAR IN UKRAINE. 42
   TAX PAYERS MONEY AND THE WAR IN ISRAEL-GAZA 45
   TRANSPARENCY AND ACCOUNTABILITY IN GOVERNMENT SPENDING 51
   CURRENCY DEVALUATION AND LOSS OF PURCHASING POWER 54
   HOW TAX LAWS INFLUENCE INFLATION? 56
   STRATEGIES FOR MITIGATING INFLATIONARY PRESSURE 58
   DO YOU HAVE ENOUGH NON-DEBT MONEY? 70
   GOVERNMENT FEES Vs TAXES 72
   THE NO-TAXES THEORY AND HOW TO MAKE IT WORK: 74
CHAPTER III 88
WORLD MACROECONOMIC OUTLOOK AND FACTS 88

2023 UNITED STATES BANKING CRISIS: 89
GLOBAL DEBT TO GDP RATIO BY COUNTRY IN 2023 98
USA DEBT TO GDP RATIO HISTORICAL 99
GLOBAL CURRENCIES Vs USD LAST 10 YEARS. 103
LIMITATIONS OF GDP AS A MEASURE OF WELL-BEING 106
GOVERNMENT ASSETS: AN UNDERUTILIZED RESOURCE 108
DOLLARIZATION OF THE ECONOMY 111
IMPLICATIONS ON THE GLOBAL ECONOMY FROM AI AND ROBOTICS. .. 114
KENYA REPLACES NUMERICAL DEBT CEILING WITH LIMIT AT 55% OF GDP
.... 117
ARGENTINA'S ECONOMIC TROUBLES. 120
A NOTE ON USA DEBT AND INTEREST PAYMENTS FOR THE YEARS TO COME 123
INTERNATIONAL TAX COMPETITIVENESS INDEX 2023 124

CHAPTER IV 129
SOME OTHER STORIES TO THINK ABOUT 129
ARGENTINAS NEW ELECTED PRESIDENT. 130
THE UAE CARBON CREDITS DEAL AHEAD COP 28 135
TAX ON JUNK AND ULTRAPROCESSED FOOD 136
WHAT ABOUT THE MOON AND SPACE EXPLORATION IMPLICATIONS? . 137
TAX EVASION PERSONALITIES 139

CONCLUSIONS 144
ABOUT THE AUTHOR 147

INTRODUCTION

In a world where financial burdens weigh heavily on individuals and nations alike, where taxes often feel like an inevitable and unyielding force, the prospect of a tax-free existence may sound like a utopian dream. Yet, as we embark on this exploration of "A Tax-Free World," we invite you to imagine the possibilities, to challenge the status quo, and to consider the profound impact that reimagining our global financial system could have on our lives and our societies.

Taxes have been a fundamental part of human civilization for centuries, serving as a means to fund governments, build infrastructure, and support societal well-being. However, the way we approach taxation and its consequences on our economies and daily lives is ripe for examination. This book ventures into the realm of tax policy, financial philosophy, and economic paradigms to unravel the intricate tapestry of taxation and, in doing so, advocates for a vision of a world that relies less on taxes and more on innovative, equitable, and sustainable financial models.

As we journey through these pages, we will explore not only the historical foundations of taxation but also the evolving landscape of global finance. We will delve into the mechanisms of taxation, its role in wealth redistribution, and the challenges it poses to economic growth and individual prosperity. We will examine the concept of a tax-free world from various angles, exploring alternative revenue sources, innovative financial instruments, and progressive policy approaches that could revolutionize the way governments generate income and provide services.

But our exploration extends beyond mere critique; it is a call to action. It is an invitation to envision a world where the burden of taxation is lighter, where individuals and businesses are empowered to thrive, and where governments are equipped to meet the needs of their citizens without overreliance on traditional tax structures. We will discuss how governments can harness the power of their assets, employ cutting-edge financial tools, and foster partnerships with the private sector to fuel economic growth and social progress.

"A Tax-Free World" is not a prescription for a one-size-fits-all solution but rather a collection of ideas, perspectives, and proposals that challenge the conventional wisdom surrounding taxation. It is a conversation starter, a catalyst for innovative thinking, and an exploration of what the future of finance could look like in a world where the burden of taxation is significantly reduced, if not eliminated.

Join us on this intellectual journey as we venture into uncharted territory, where the rules of the financial game are rewritten, and where the quest for a tax-free world is more than a vision—it's a compelling possibility that could reshape the way we live, work, and prosper.

CHAPTER I

WHERE WE COME FROM AND WHERE WE ARE NOW.

WHAT IS THE HISTORY ON TAXES, WHERE THEY COME FROM?

The history of taxes is a long and complex one, dating back thousands of years. Taxes have been a fundamental part of human civilization, and they have evolved in various forms and purposes over time. Here is a brief overview of the history of taxes:

Ancient Civilizations:

Taxes have been collected since ancient times. In ancient Egypt, for example, taxes were collected in the form of agricultural produce, labor, or goods.

In ancient Rome, taxes known as "centesima rerum venalium" were imposed on the sale of goods, while "centesima rerum rusticarum" were levied on agricultural products.

Medieval Period:

During the Middle Ages, feudal systems prevailed in many parts of the world. Lords and monarchs collected taxes in the form of agricultural products, labor, or military service from their subjects.

The Catholic Church also collected tithes, which were a form of religious tax.

Renaissance and Early Modern Era:

The development of modern states in Europe saw the emergence of more systematic taxation systems. Taxes were often collected to fund wars and state-building efforts.

In England, the Magna Carta of 1215 limited the power of the king to levy taxes without the consent of the nobility.

Colonial America:

The American colonies were subject to taxation by the British government in the 18th century. Taxes like the Stamp Act and the Tea Act led to colonial unrest and contributed to the American Revolution.

Modern Taxation Systems:

The 19th and 20th centuries saw the development of modern tax systems in many countries, including the income tax. The United States introduced its first income tax in the 1860s during the Civil War and later ratified the 16th Amendment in 1913 to establish a federal income tax.

World Wars and Post-War Period:

Both World War I and World War II necessitated significant increases in taxation to fund the war efforts.

After World War II, many countries, including the United States, expanded their social welfare programs and increased taxes to finance them.

Globalization and Taxation:

In the modern era, globalization has created complex challenges for taxation. Corporations and individuals often engage in international financial activities that can be subject to various tax jurisdictions.

Types of Taxes:

Taxes come in various forms, including income taxes, sales taxes, property taxes, excise taxes, corporate taxes, and more.

The purposes of taxes can range from funding government services and infrastructure to addressing income inequality and promoting social welfare.

Throughout history, taxes have been a source of revenue for governments to carry out essential functions and address societal needs. However, the types, rates, and methods of taxation have evolved over time, reflecting changes in economic, political, and social contexts. Today, tax systems are complex and vary widely from one country to another, and taxation remains a key element of government finance and public policy worldwide.

THE ROLE OF TAXES IN MODERN SOCIETIES?

Taxes play a multifaceted and crucial role in modern societies, serving as a fundamental mechanism for governments to generate revenue and accomplish various economic, social, and political objectives. Here are the key roles of taxes in modern societies:

Revenue Generation:

The primary function of taxes is to provide governments with the necessary funds to finance public services and infrastructure, such as healthcare, education, transportation, defense, and law enforcement.

Tax revenue is vital for maintaining and improving a nation's physical and social infrastructure, which, in turn, supports economic growth and societal well-being.

Income Redistribution:

Taxes can be used to address income inequality by collecting a greater percentage of income from higher earners through progressive taxation. These funds can then be redistributed through social programs and benefits to support lower-income individuals and families.

Social safety nets, such as welfare programs and unemployment benefits, are funded by tax revenue and serve as mechanisms for wealth redistribution.

Economic Stabilization:

Taxes can be adjusted during economic downturns to stimulate or stabilize the economy. For instance, governments may lower taxes to encourage consumer spending or increase government spending through fiscal policies during recessions.

Progressive taxation can also help reduce income disparities, which can contribute to economic stability.

Public Goods and Services:

Taxes enable governments to provide essential public goods and services that may not be efficiently provided by the private sector, such as national defense, public education, healthcare infrastructure, and environmental protection.

Regulation and Incentives:

Tax policy can be used to shape behavior and promote specific societal goals. For example, governments often use tax incentives to encourage investments in renewable energy, research and development, or affordable housing.

Taxes can also be used to discourage undesirable behaviors, such as tobacco or alcohol consumption, by imposing excise taxes.

Public Policy Goals:

Taxation can be a tool to support broader public policy objectives, such as environmental conservation, by taxing carbon emissions or other pollutants.

Governments can also use taxes to encourage sustainable practices and discourage harmful activities.

Infrastructure Investment:

Taxes fund the construction and maintenance of essential infrastructure, including roads, bridges, public transportation, and utilities. These investments support economic growth and quality of life.

Legal Framework:

Taxes provide a legal framework for a nation's financial operations. They define who is subject to taxation, the types of taxes imposed, and the rates at which they are levied.

Taxes also establish accountability by requiring governments to report on their revenue collection and spending.

Social Contract:

Taxation is often seen as part of the social contract between citizens and the government. Citizens contribute taxes in exchange for public services, protection, and the rule of law.

Democratic Representation:

In democratic societies, tax policies are typically determined by elected representatives. Citizens have a voice in shaping tax laws and policies through their elected officials.

In summary, taxes are a fundamental aspect of modern societies, serving as a financial backbone that enables governments to provide public goods, support economic stability, address social inequalities, and pursue various policy objectives. The role of taxes is complex and multifaceted, and their design and implementation have a profound impact on the economic and social fabric of a nation.

USD CURRENCY HISTORY AND WORLD IMPACT.

The history of the United States Dollar (USD) is a story of monetary evolution and its profound impact on the world. Here is a brief overview of the USD's history and its global significance:

Early History:

The United States adopted the dollar as its official currency in 1792. The U.S. Constitution gave Congress the power to coin money and regulate its value.

The first U.S. mint was established in Philadelphia in 1792, producing coins with denominations like the dollar, cent, and dime.

19th Century:

During the 19th century, the United States experienced rapid westward expansion and economic growth. The dollar played a crucial role in facilitating trade and commerce across the expanding nation.

The Gold Rushes of the mid-19th century led to the minting of gold coins, further strengthening the USD's role as a global currency.

Civil War Era:

The American Civil War (1861-1865) led to the issuance of paper currency, known as "greenbacks," to finance the war effort. This marked a significant step in the development of U.S. paper money.

20th Century:

In 1913, the Federal Reserve System was established as the central banking system of the United States. It had the authority to issue and regulate the currency.

The U.S. went through two World Wars and a Great Depression in the first half of the 20th century. The USD remained relatively stable and gained trust globally, becoming a preferred reserve currency.

Bretton Woods Agreement (1944):

After World War II, the U.S. played a leading role in establishing the Bretton Woods Agreement, which pegged the value of most world currencies to the USD, which was backed by gold at $35 per ounce. This made the USD the world's primary reserve currency.

The Bretton Woods system facilitated international trade and financial stability for several decades.

End of the Gold Standard (1971):

In 1971, President Richard Nixon suspended the convertibility of the USD into gold, effectively ending the Bretton Woods system. This event, known as the "Nixon Shock," marked the USD's transition to a fiat currency not backed by a physical commodity.

The USD's value became determined by supply and demand in international markets.

Modern Era:

The USD has remained the world's dominant reserve currency due to the size and stability of the U.S. economy, as well as the liquidity of USD-denominated assets.

The global financial system relies on the USD for international trade, commodity pricing, and as a store of value.

U.S. government debt, in the form of U.S. Treasury securities, is considered one of the safest investments worldwide, attracting global investors.

Impact on the World:

The USD's status as the world's primary reserve currency gives the U.S. significant economic and geopolitical influence.

The USD's use in international trade simplifies transactions and reduces exchange rate risk for global businesses.

Many countries hold significant foreign exchange reserves in USD, which provides stability in times of economic uncertainty.

The U.S. can borrow at lower interest rates due to the global demand for its currency, enabling it to finance government operations and invest in infrastructure and social programs.

In summary, the history of the USD is closely tied to the economic and political development of the United States. Its status as the world's dominant reserve currency has had a profound impact on the global economy and international financial system, making it a key player in the world's economic stability and prosperity.

World reserve currency periods:

- Egypt (3150 BC-1200 BC)

- Lydia (1200BC-550BC)

- Achaemenid Empire (550BC-330BC)

- Macedonia (330BC-315BC)

- Seleucid Empire (315BC - 200BC)

- Rome (200 BC-395 AD)

- Byzantine Empire (395-660 & 750-1200)

- Umayyad Caliphate (660-750)

- Florence & Venice (1200-1450)

- Portugal (1450–1530)

- Spain (1530–1640)

- Netherlands (1640–1720)

- France (1720–1815)

- Great Britain (1815–1920)

- United States (1921-2030)

*- Bitcoin (2030-forever)

*Bitcoin has been seen as flight to quality within the latest few years. Given all the benefits and advantages that people sees in it as being decentralized and fixed limited supply. Not like FIAT currency which tends to devaluate and loose value via inflation.

THE EURO AND ITS HISTORY.

The Euro (€) is the official currency of the Eurozone, which is a group of 19 of the 27 European Union (EU) member states that have adopted the euro as their official currency. The Eurozone countries are bound by a common monetary policy, and the euro is managed by the European Central Bank (ECB). Here is an overview of the Euro's history:

1. Pre-Euro Currency Arrangements:

Before the euro, European countries used various national currencies. Exchange rate fluctuations and the costs associated with currency conversions were seen as barriers to economic integration within the EU.

2. Maastricht Treaty (1992):

The Maastricht Treaty, officially known as the Treaty on European Union, was signed in 1992 and laid the groundwork for the establishment of the euro. It outlined the criteria that EU member states needed to meet to adopt the single currency.

3. Euro Established (1999):

The euro was introduced as an electronic currency for banking and financial transactions on January 1, 1999. During this phase, it existed as a virtual currency, and only non-cash transactions were conducted in euros. Exchange rates between the participating currencies were irrevocably fixed.

4. Euro Banknotes and Coins (2002):

Euro banknotes and coins were introduced on January 1, 2002, marking the physical introduction of the currency to the public. People could use euros for daily transactions, and national currencies were gradually phased out.

5. Eurozone Expansion:

The Eurozone started with 11 member states: Austria, Belgium, Finland, France, Germany, Ireland, Italy, Luxembourg, Netherlands, Portugal, and Spain. Greece joined in 2001, and subsequent expansions brought the total to 19 countries by 2023.

6. Euro Banknotes and Coins Design:

Euro banknotes and coins feature designs that represent architectural styles from different periods in European history. Each denomination has its own color and depicts a particular era.

7. European Central Bank (ECB):

The ECB, based in Frankfurt, Germany, is responsible for monetary policy in the Eurozone. It aims to maintain price stability and control inflation. The Eurosystem, comprising the central banks of the Eurozone countries and the ECB, manages the euro.

8. Euro as a Global Reserve Currency:

The euro is one of the world's major reserve currencies, alongside the U.S. dollar. It is used in international trade and finance and held in significant amounts by central banks around the world.

9. Economic Challenges:

The Eurozone has faced economic challenges, including the global financial crisis of 2008, the sovereign debt crisis in some member states, and divergent economic performance among Eurozone countries.

10. Brexit (2020):

- The United Kingdom, which was part of the EU, officially left the EU on January 31, 2020. However, the euro is not the official currency in the UK, and it continues to use the British pound.

The euro has played a significant role in fostering economic integration among European countries. However, challenges such as economic disparities among member states and differing fiscal policies continue to be subjects of discussion and debate within the Eurozone.

The European Union tax system and how it works.

The tax systems within the European Union (EU) are diverse, as each member state maintains its own sovereign fiscal policies. While the EU provides a framework for economic cooperation, including some coordination on tax matters, tax policies and rates vary significantly from one member state to another. Here are key aspects of the tax system within the EU:

1. National Sovereignty:

Taxation is a matter of national sovereignty, meaning that each EU member state has the authority to set its own tax policies, rates, and rules. This has led to a wide range of tax systems across the EU.

2. Common VAT System:

One area of harmonization is the Value Added Tax (VAT) system. Member states follow common rules for VAT, ensuring a degree of consistency in how this consumption tax is applied across the EU.

3. Coordination on Corporate Taxation:

While there is no common corporate tax rate in the EU, there has been some effort to coordinate corporate taxation policies. Discussions about a common consolidated corporate tax base (CCCTB) have taken place, aiming to simplify tax compliance for multinational corporations operating in multiple EU countries.

4. Savings Tax Directive:

The Savings Tax Directive is an agreement among EU member states to exchange information on the savings income of individuals. This directive aims to prevent tax evasion by individuals who earn interest income in a different EU member state than their residence.

5. Common Market and Free Movement:

The EU's common market and the principle of free movement of goods, services, capital, and people mean that tax matters are closely linked to economic integration. Businesses and individuals can operate across borders, and tax implications play a role in decisions on where to establish businesses, invest, or reside.

6. Challenges of Tax Competition:

Tax competition among EU member states is a notable feature. Some countries offer lower corporate tax rates or specific tax incentives to attract businesses and investments. This competition can lead to concerns about tax base erosion and profit shifting.

7. Anti-Tax Avoidance Directive (ATAD):

The EU has taken steps to combat tax avoidance with the Anti-Tax Avoidance Directive (ATAD). The directive includes measures to address hybrid mismatches, interest deductibility, controlled foreign company rules, and other aspects of corporate taxation.

8. Eurozone Coordination:

Eurozone countries, which share the euro as their common currency, have a higher degree of economic coordination, including discussions on fiscal matters. However, significant differences in tax policies still exist among Eurozone members.

9. Bilateral Tax Treaties:

Many EU member states have bilateral tax treaties with each other to avoid double taxation and facilitate cooperation. These treaties define which country has the primary right to tax specific types of income.

10. Future Developments:

- Ongoing discussions within the EU include proposals for further tax harmonization, such as the digital tax and minimum effective tax rate for corporations, aiming to ensure a fair distribution of taxation in the digital economy.

In summary, the tax system in the EU is characterized by a balance between national sovereignty and efforts to coordinate certain aspects of taxation. While there are common elements, significant diversity exists among member states' tax policies and systems. Ongoing discussions and initiatives aim to address challenges and promote fair and efficient taxation within the EU.

BRIEF HISTORY ON TRADE AND PAYMENTS:

In the early days of human civilization, trade and payments were conducted in ways that were quite different from the modern global economy. Here's an overview of how trade and payments were made in ancient times:

Barter System:

One of the earliest forms of trade was the barter system, where goods and services were exchanged directly without a standardized medium of exchange like money.

People would trade goods they had in surplus for items they needed. For example, a farmer might exchange a portion of their grain for clothing or tools produced by another individual.

Commodity Money:

As societies developed, the barter system became less practical because of the limitations in finding mutually beneficial exchanges. This led to the emergence of commodity money.

Commodity money consisted of items with intrinsic value, such as grain, cattle, or precious metals like gold and silver. These commodities were widely accepted in trade because they had inherent worth.

Cowry Shells:

In various parts of the world, including Africa, Asia, and the Pacific Islands, cowry shells were used as a form of money. These small, durable shells were easily transportable and recognized as a valuable medium of exchange.

Metal Coins:

The use of metal coins as a form of money became more prevalent in ancient societies. Coins were often made from metals like gold, silver, copper, and bronze.

The Lydians in Anatolia (modern-day Turkey) are often credited with producing the first standardized metal coins around the 7th century BCE.

Trade Routes and Caravans:

Trade between different regions often occurred along established trade routes. These routes facilitated the exchange of goods and ideas across vast distances.

Caravans, comprised of traders and pack animals like camels, played a crucial role in transporting goods along these routes, such as the Silk Road in Asia and the Trans-Saharan trade routes in Africa.

Silk Road:

The Silk Road was a network of trade routes connecting East Asia to the Mediterranean, facilitating the exchange of goods like silk, spices, precious metals, and cultural knowledge between civilizations.

Trade and Cultural Exchange:

Trade in ancient times not only involved the exchange of physical goods but also cultural diffusion. It led to the spread of ideas, religions, languages, and innovations.

Local Markets:

Local markets and bazaars were common in ancient cities and towns. These markets allowed for the exchange of a wide variety of goods and served as centers of economic activity and social interaction.

Early Banking and Credit:

In some ancient civilizations, rudimentary banking and credit systems emerged. For example, the Mesopotamians developed clay tablets as early forms of financial records and credit agreements.

Coinage by Rulers:

Many rulers and emperors in ancient times issued their own coinage, often featuring their likeness. These coins were used not only for trade but also as a means of spreading political propaganda.

Trade and payment systems in ancient times were diverse and adapted to the specific needs and resources of each civilization. While these early systems lacked the sophistication of modern financial systems, they laid the foundation for the development of currency, banking, and international trade that would become integral to today's global economy.

An island in the Pacific called Yap.

There is an island in the Pacific called Yap that uses circular stones as currency. The stones are too large to move so the ownership of the stones is passed by word of mouth to transact business.

Economists love the tiny island called Yap located in the Pacific Ocean, because it helps answer this really basic question: what is money?

There's no gold or silver on Yap. But hundreds of years ago, explorers from the island found limestone deposits on another island hundreds of miles away. And they carved this limestone into huge stone discs, which they brought back across the sea on their small bamboo boats.

It is not clear if these stones began a currently immediately, but at some point in time the people on Yap realized what most societies realize. They needed something that everyone agrees you can use to pay for stuff.

Like every society, the people of Yap took the thing they considered precious — their version of gold — and decided that was money.

There was just one key thing about this money: it was really heavy. A big piece could weigh more than a car.

They ended up talking about the stones themselves not changing hands at all. One person gives it to another person. But the stone doesn't move. It's just that everybody in the village knows the stone now has a new owner.

The stone doesn't even need to be on the island to count as money.

One time, according to the island's oral tradition, a crew was bringing a stone coin back to Yap on a boat. Due to a storm, the stone sank. The crew made it back to Yap and told everybody what happened.

And everybody decided that the piece of stone at the bottom of the ocean was still good.

This system, in the end, feels really familiar. If you go online to pay your electric bill, what's the difference with the stones?

The Yap islands group is part of Micronesia and has a very peculiar currency: stone. Stone money known as "Rai" are large stone disks, sometimes measuring up to 4 meters, with a hole in the middle that was used for carrying them. Rai was and is still used as a trading currency there.

CHAPTER II
MY MACROECONOMIC THEORY

THE CONCEPT OF A TAX-FREE WORLD.

The concept of a Tax-Free World is an intriguing and often debated idea that envisions a society or global economy in which traditional forms of taxation, such as income taxes, sales taxes, and property taxes, are significantly reduced or even eliminated. While this concept is not currently a reality, it sparks important discussions about the role of taxation in society and the potential benefits and challenges associated with reducing or eliminating taxes.

Here are some key aspects of the concept of a Tax-Free World:

1. Financing through Alternative Means:

Proponents of a Tax-Free World argue that governments should explore alternative sources of revenue to fund public services and infrastructure. These alternatives might include user fees, government-owned enterprises, or revenue generated from government investments.

2. Reducing the Burden on Individuals and Businesses:

One of the main appeals of a Tax-Free World is the idea of relieving individuals and businesses from the financial burden of paying taxes. This could potentially stimulate economic growth and encourage entrepreneurship.

3. Simplification of Tax Systems:

A Tax-Free World might involve simplifying complex tax systems, which can be costly to administer and can create compliance challenges for individuals and businesses.

4. Social and Economic Impacts:

Advocates argue that a Tax-Free World could lead to increased disposable income for individuals and reduced operating costs for businesses. This, in turn, could stimulate consumer spending, investment and at the same time not putting pressure on inflation from government side.

5. Potential Challenges:

Critics of the Tax-Free World concept raise concerns about how governments would finance essential public services, such as education, healthcare, infrastructure, and defense, without tax revenue. They also question the fairness of such a system, as it may disproportionately benefit the wealthy.

6. Transitioning to a Tax-Free World:

Transitioning to a Tax-Free World would require careful planning and consideration of alternative revenue sources. Governments might need to explore options like natural resource royalties, sovereign wealth funds, or value-added taxes to replace lost tax revenue.

7. Global Cooperation:

Achieving a Tax-Free World on a global scale would likely require international cooperation and coordination to address potential issues related to tax evasion, trade imbalances, and global economic stability.

It's essential to note that the idea of a Tax-Free World is often presented as an aspirational concept rather than a practical policy proposal in most discussions. In practice, governments rely on tax revenue to fund essential public services, maintain infrastructure, and address income inequality. While there may be room for tax reform and simplification, completely eliminating taxes remains a complex and challenging proposition that would require careful consideration of its implications on society and the economy.

WHY SOME COUNTRIES DON'T RELY ON TAXES AND WHICH ONES?

Some countries have managed to minimize or even eliminate their reliance on certain types of taxes, particularly income taxes. The specific reasons for this vary from one country to another and often depend on their unique economic and political circumstances. Here are a few examples of countries that have limited or no income tax and the reasons behind their approach:

United Arab Emirates (UAE): The UAE is known for its tax-friendly environment, including the absence of personal income tax. The country generates revenue primarily from other sources, such as oil exports, tourism, and business-related fees. The UAE's wealth from oil resources has allowed it to forgo income taxes and attract foreign investment and expatriate workers.

Dubai's economic model is often described as a tax-friendly environment, where individuals and businesses benefit from a low-tax or tax-free regime. While it is true that Dubai and the broader United Arab Emirates (UAE) have a unique tax system, it's important to clarify some aspects of their economic model:

No Personal Income Tax: One of the key features of Dubai's tax system is the absence of personal income tax. Individuals are not required to pay income tax on their earnings, which can attract talented professionals and entrepreneurs to live and work in Dubai.

Limited Corporate Taxation: Dubai has implemented a corporate tax rate of 0% for many industries, making it an attractive destination for businesses. However, certain sectors may be subject to specific taxes, such as the oil and banking sectors.

Business-Friendly Policies: Dubai has implemented various policies and initiatives to create a favorable business environment. This includes streamlined bureaucracy, simplified regulations, free trade zones, and incentives for foreign direct investment. These measures have contributed to attracting businesses and promoting economic growth.

Revenue from Other Sources: While Dubai relies less on traditional taxes, it generates revenue through other means. For example, the government collects fees and duties on services, licenses, property transactions, and tourism-related activities. Additionally, Dubai's economy benefits from industries such as real estate, tourism, trade, finance, and transportation.

Economic Diversification: Dubai has been actively diversifying its economy to reduce dependence on oil and embrace other sectors. This strategy has included investments in areas such as tourism, hospitality, finance, technology, and renewable energy. By diversifying its economic base, Dubai aims to ensure long-term sustainability and resilience.

It's important to note that Dubai's economic model is unique and specific to its local context. While the absence of certain taxes may attract businesses and individuals, there are other factors at play in Dubai's economic success, including strategic investments, infrastructure development, government support, and a strategic geographic location.

Furthermore, it's worth mentioning that the UAE as a whole has implemented a Value Added Tax (VAT) system. Since January 2018, VAT has been imposed on certain goods and services across the UAE, including Dubai. This move has diversified the government's revenue sources and supported public services and infrastructure development.

Overall, Dubai's economic sustainability without traditional taxation is a result of a combination of factors, including a business-friendly environment, diversification efforts, strategic investments, and revenue generation from alternative sources.

Saudi Arabia: Like the UAE, Saudi Arabia relies heavily on revenue from its vast oil reserves. It has no personal income tax, and the government primarily funds its operations through oil sales. However, the Saudi government has introduced other forms of taxation, such as a value-added tax (VAT), to diversify its revenue sources.

Monaco: Monaco, a small city-state on the French Riviera, is famous for its lack of personal income tax. The principality generates income through tourism, banking, and other financial services. It can afford to have no income tax due to its small size, high concentration of wealthy residents, and revenue from other sectors.

Bahrain: Bahrain is another Gulf state that does not levy personal income tax. Instead, it generates income from oil and gas production, financial services, and tourism. Bahrain's government has implemented other taxes, such as a corporate income tax and a VAT, to diversify revenue sources.

Brunei: Brunei, a small Southeast Asian nation, does not impose personal income tax on its citizens. The country's revenue primarily comes from its oil and natural gas reserves. However, Brunei has introduced other taxes and fees to reduce its dependence on oil exports.

Panama: Taxes in Panama are relatively straightforward compared to many other countries, and the country is known for its favorable tax policies. Here is an overview of how taxes work in Panama:

Territorial Tax System:

Panama follows a territorial tax system. This means that taxes are levied on income generated within Panama's borders but not on income earned abroad. Foreign-source income is generally not subject to taxation in Panama.

Income Tax:

Panama has a progressive income tax system with different tax rates depending on the level of income. The tax rates for individuals range from 0% to 25%.

Income tax in Panama is only applied to income earned within the country. Foreign-source income, including income from foreign investments and foreign pensions, is exempt from Panamanian income tax.

Value Added Tax (VAT):

Panama has a Value Added Tax (VAT) system known as the ITBMS (Impuesto de Transferencia de Bienes Corporales Muebles y la Prestación de Servicios). The standard VAT rate is 7%. Some basic goods and services, such as certain food items, medicines, and healthcare services, are exempt from VAT.

Property Tax:

Property tax rates in Panama vary depending on the value and location of the property. The tax rate typically ranges from 0.6% to 2.1% of the registered property value. Some properties, such as newly constructed homes, may be exempt from property tax for a limited period.

Capital Gains Tax:

As of my last knowledge update in September 2021, Panama does not have a specific capital gains tax. However, gains from the sale of real estate may be subject to a transfer tax known as the ITBMS, which is generally 2% of the sale price.

Gains from the sale of securities and financial assets are typically not subject to tax.

Corporate Tax:

Panama imposes corporate income tax on companies operating within its borders. The standard corporate income tax rate is 25%.

Foreign-source income earned by Panamanian companies is generally exempt from corporate income tax.

Tax Treaties:

Panama has signed tax treaties with several countries to avoid double taxation and promote international cooperation in tax matters. These treaties may affect the taxation of certain types of income for residents of those countries.

Tax Reporting and Compliance:

Individuals and businesses in Panama are required to file tax returns and comply with tax regulations. The tax year in Panama is typically the calendar year.

Panama has introduced measures to enhance tax transparency and combat tax evasion, including participation in the Common Reporting Standard (CRS).

Tax Incentives:

Panama offers various tax incentives to attract foreign investment and promote specific industries, such as tourism and agriculture. These incentives may include exemptions from certain taxes or reduced tax rates for a specified period.

It's essential to note that tax laws and regulations can change over time, so it's advisable to consult with a local tax advisor or legal expert in Panama to ensure compliance with the latest tax requirements.

The economy of Panama is characterized by a unique combination of services, trade, and a strategic location that makes it a key player in the global economy. Here is an overview of how the Panama economy works:

Geographic Advantage:

Panama's geographic location is its most significant economic asset. The country serves as a bridge between North and South America and is home to the Panama Canal, a vital maritime route connecting the Atlantic and Pacific Oceans.

The Panama Canal is a major source of revenue for the country, generating income through tolls paid by shipping companies and serving as a conduit for international trade.

Services Sector:

The services sector is the largest component of Panama's economy, contributing significantly to GDP. Key elements of this sector include:

Financial Services: Panama is a major international financial center, known for its banking and offshore services. It has a robust banking sector that attracts foreign investments.

Shipping and Logistics: Beyond the Panama Canal, Panama's strategic location has fostered the development of a robust shipping and logistics industry, including ports, free trade zones, and transportation services.

Tourism: Panama's natural beauty, historical sites, and cultural attractions draw tourists. The country offers a range of tourism-related services, including hospitality, transportation, and ecotourism activities.

Real Estate and Construction: Infrastructure development, including the construction of commercial and residential properties, has been a prominent sector in Panama's economy.

Trade and Commerce:

Panama's open and liberal trade policies have made it a regional hub for trade. The Colón Free Trade Zone, located near the Atlantic entrance of the Panama Canal, is one of the largest free trade zones in the Americas, facilitating trade in a wide range of goods. The country's favorable trade agreements, including a Free Trade Agreement with the United States, encourage foreign investment and trade relations.

Agriculture and Manufacturing:

While the services sector dominates the economy, Panama also has an agricultural and manufacturing base. Key agricultural exports include bananas, coffee, and sugar. The manufacturing sector produces goods such as clothing, processed foods, and beverages.

Government Revenue:

The Panama Canal Authority generates substantial revenue from toll collections, which contributes significantly to the government's budget.

Panama's government revenue is also supported by taxes, including income taxes and consumption taxes.

Currency and Monetary Policy:

Panama uses the U.S. dollar as its official currency. The government does not issue its own currency, which provides economic stability and encourages foreign investment.

Economic Growth and Development:

Panama has experienced robust economic growth in recent years, driven by its services sector and infrastructure development.

The government has invested in infrastructure projects, including the expansion of the Panama Canal, which has further boosted economic activity and trade.

Challenges and Inequality:

Despite its economic growth, Panama faces challenges related to income inequality and poverty. While urban areas have prospered, rural areas often have lower living standards.

There are ongoing efforts to address social and economic disparities and promote inclusive growth.

In summary, Panama's economy is characterized by its strategic location, a strong services sector, trade-oriented policies, and a focus on international finance and logistics. The Panama Canal remains a cornerstone of its economic success, facilitating global trade and contributing significantly to the country's revenue. However, Panama also faces challenges related to economic inequality and social development, which policymakers are actively addressing.

It's important to note that while these countries do not rely on personal income tax, they may have other types of taxes, such as corporate income tax, value-added tax (VAT), or other levies, to generate revenue. Additionally, the ability to forgo income tax often depends on the presence of alternative revenue streams, such as natural resources, tourism, or financial services, which can fund government operations and services.

Each country's taxation policy is influenced by its unique economic circumstances, government priorities, and the need to attract foreign investment and talent. Additionally, tax policies can change over time in response to evolving economic and political factors.

NOTABLE MISUSES OF TAXPAYER FUNDS:

Notable misuses of taxpayer funds have occurred in various countries and contexts, often leading to public outrage, investigations, and calls for greater accountability. Here are some case studies of notable misuses of taxpayer funds:

Watergate Scandal (United States, 1970s):

The Watergate scandal is one of the most infamous cases of misuse of government funds and power. It involved a break-in at the Democratic National Committee headquarters in the Watergate complex in Washington, D.C., by individuals connected to President Richard Nixon's re-election campaign. Taxpayer funds were misused for illegal activities, including the break-in and efforts to cover it up. The scandal ultimately led to President Nixon's resignation in 1974.

Enron Scandal (United States, 2001):

While not directly a misuse of taxpayer funds, the Enron scandal involved fraudulent financial practices by the Enron Corporation, which led to the company's collapse. Enron manipulated accounting procedures to hide its financial troubles, resulting in massive losses for shareholders, employees, and pension funds.

The scandal revealed weaknesses in regulatory oversight and corporate governance, leading to calls for reform in financial reporting and auditing practices.

Indian 2G Spectrum Scandal (India, 2008):

The 2G spectrum scandal involved the alleged underpricing of 2G mobile phone licenses by the Indian government, leading to a significant loss of potential revenue for the treasury. The government was accused of selling licenses at far below market value.

The scandal resulted in a public outcry, legal investigations, and the cancellation of licenses. Several prominent politicians and business leaders faced charges and were convicted in connection with the case.

Angola's "Dos Santos Files" (Angola, 2020):

In 2020, investigative journalists uncovered alleged embezzlement and misuse of public funds by members of Angola's ruling elite, including former President José Eduardo dos Santos and his family.

The leaked documents, known as the "Dos Santos Files," revealed the alleged diversion of millions of dollars in state funds into offshore accounts and private business ventures, highlighting the challenges of corruption and mismanagement in the country.

Malaysia's 1MDB Scandal (Malaysia, ongoing):

The 1Malaysia Development Berhad (1MDB) scandal involved the alleged embezzlement of billions of dollars from a state investment fund. The funds were reportedly misappropriated for personal gain by individuals connected to former Prime Minister Najib Razak.

The scandal has led to legal action in multiple countries, including the United States, and has had political and financial repercussions in Malaysia.

These case studies illustrate the serious consequences of misusing taxpayer funds, including erosion of public trust, legal action, and financial losses. They also underscore the importance of transparency, accountability, and robust oversight mechanisms to prevent and address such abuses.

Colombia's president and vice president spending scandal. (Ongoing):

Currently Colombians have been fighting over the media the way and on what tax payer's funds are being used by their top rulers.

For example The Vise president of the country she is travelling all the time in a military Helicopter to move around, even to go and buy groceries and attend small meetings. The claim it is that this is not necessary, too expensive. That helicopter can be of a better use and the money spent on gas also could be used in many other activities to help people.

Her answer to this is: demalas, pueden llorar! (just bad luck and you can also cry about it).

The president calling for protests or political parades to support them. Bringing indigenous people, just to mention one group, to the capital, Bogota, form various parts of the country in large buses and giving them lunch. Same as all the required infrastructure around it in sound equipment, coverage, tents, food, transport, free concerts, and many other logistic matters for just one-day rally to come and support the actual elected government.

Taking his daughter in Walt Disney and Orlando parks using the presidential plane, just for that. Also many other international trips and travel without much political goals or fundament with his family.

These are all claims made public on media platforms and newspapers within the country.

TAX PAYERS AND THE WAR IN UKRAINE.

The United States had provided various forms of financial assistance to Ukraine. These forms of assistance included military aid, humanitarian aid, economic assistance, and support for democratic and governance reforms. However, please note that the situation may have evolved since then, and it's essential to check the latest news and official government sources for the most up-to-date information on U.S. assistance to Ukraine.

Here are some key points related to U.S. financial assistance to Ukraine:

Military Aid: The United States has provided military assistance to Ukraine to support its defense capabilities. This aid has included items such as lethal weapons, non-lethal military equipment, and training for Ukrainian armed forces.

Humanitarian Aid: The U.S. government has provided humanitarian assistance to address the needs of internally displaced persons (IDPs) and vulnerable populations affected by the conflict in eastern Ukraine. This assistance includes food aid, medical supplies, and support for humanitarian organizations.

Economic Assistance: The United States has offered economic support to Ukraine to help stabilize its economy, address economic reforms, and promote economic development. This assistance has included loan guarantees and financial aid packages.

Democracy and Governance Support: The U.S. has provided assistance to Ukraine to strengthen democratic institutions, promote the rule of law, combat corruption, and support civil society organizations. These efforts aim to help Ukraine build a more transparent and accountable government.

Energy Sector Support: Given Ukraine's energy challenges, the U.S. has also supported reforms in the country's energy sector. This support includes initiatives to improve energy efficiency, diversify energy sources, and enhance energy security.

International Organizations: The U.S. has contributed funds to international organizations, such as the United Nations and the Organization for Security and Co-operation in Europe (OSCE), to support their efforts related to Ukraine.

The exact amount of U.S. financial assistance to Ukraine can vary from year to year and depends on various factors, including legislative appropriations and geopolitical developments.

For the most current information on U.S. assistance to Ukraine, you can refer to official statements from the U.S. Department of State, the U.S. Agency for International Development (USAID), and other relevant U.S. government agencies. Additionally, you may find updates in news reports and official statements from the Ukrainian government.

The war in Ukraine has become a frequent target for commentators who believe that U.S. spending toward the conflict ought to be curbed and reinvested domestically.

The two frontrunners in early polls for the 2024 Republican presidential contenders, former President Donald Trump and Florida Governor Ron DeSantis—who hasn't declared yet but is expected to run—have both said they don't see Ukraine as a vital national strategic interest for the U.S.

Amid this criticism, a figure of $200 billion has been repeatedly quoted as the U.S. total spending toward the country, reportedly its entire GDP.

A tweet by former Assistant Secretary for Public Affairs for the U.S. Department of the Treasury Monica Crowley, posted on April 18, 2023, viewed 32,000 times, stated: "$200 billion+ of your hard-earned money has been disappeared into the corrupt money-pit of Ukraine.

"Happy Tax Day!"

This figure has been repeated by a number of right-leaning politicians and public figures in the past two months including Representative Andy Biggs (R-

AZ), former Trump advisor Steve Bannon, and former Republican candidate for Arizona governor Kari Lake.

A February 12, 2023, article by Fox News was among its first appearances, with the authors noting two sources: the presidential office of Ukraine and the Ukraine Support Tracker (produced by economic research organization the Kiel Institute for the World Economy).

However, the Kiel Institute states U.S. spending on all categories of aid has reached around $77 billion, not $200 billion, enacted across four bills since February 2022.

In total, Congress has allocated $113 billion in a combination of mostly military, government, and humanitarian aid to Ukraine since last year, according to the Department of Defense Office of Inspector General.

But, Kiel notes that a "large portion" of this $113 billion "will not flow directly to Ukraine but is instead allocated towards a broad variety of spending purposes."

Source: https://www.newsweek.com/fact-check-have-us-taxpayers-sent-200-billion-ukraine-1796322

WASHINGTON -- The Pentagon said Tuesday that it overestimated the value of the weapons it has sent to Ukraine by $6.2 billion over the past two years — about double early estimates — resulting in a surplus that will be used for future security packages.

Pentagon spokeswoman Sabrina Singh said a detailed review of the accounting error found that the military services used replacement costs rather than the book value of equipment that was pulled from Pentagon stocks and sent to Ukraine. She said final calculations show there was an error of $3.6 billion in the current fiscal year and $2.6 billion in the 2022 fiscal year, which ended last Sept. 30.

As a result, the department now has additional money in its coffers to use to support Ukraine as it pursues its counteroffensive against Russia. And it come as the fiscal year is wrapping up and congressional funding was beginning to dwindle.

Source: https://abcnews.go.com/US/wireStory/pentagon-accounting-error-extra-62-billion-ukraine-military-100254358

TAX PAYERS MONEY AND THE WAR IN ISRAEL-GAZA

How Much Aid Does the U.S. Give to Israel?

The United States has given Israel more aid than any other nation since World War II, granting it more than $260 billion.

Calls for more aid to Israel came quickly in the wake of a terrorist attack by Hamas on the country this weekend, and President Biden has said military assistance is on its way. The USS Gerald R. Ford, the Navy's newest and most advanced aircraft carrier, has already been dispatched to the region, and more aid in the form of equipment, resources and munitions is expected to arrive in coming days.

The U.S. commitment to aiding Israel has long-standing roots. The United States has given Israel more than $260 billion in combined military and economic aid since World War II, plus about $10 billion more in contributions for missile defense systems like the Iron Dome, a U.S. News analysis finds. That's the most granted to any country throughout that time frame, and around $100 billion more than Egypt, the second-highest recipient historically.

For nearly three decades – from fiscal years 1974 to 2002 – Israel was the top recipient of U.S. aid, the longest-standing duration for a top aid recipient dating back to 1946, according to figures from ForeignAssistance.gov. While 2003 to 2020 saw the most aid going to either Iraq or Afghanistan, Israel nevertheless remained a top three aid recipient throughout that time.

U.S. Aid to Israel Since 1951

Israel was the top recipient of combined U.S. economic and military aid from fiscal years **1974-2002** and in **2021**. It has been a top-three recipient since 1971.

In 2021, U.S. obligations to Israel amounted to $3.31 billion, a figure that saw Israel returning to the top spot among aid recipients that year. But in 2022, the U.S. committed $12 billion to Ukraine in its defense against Russia's invasion, far exceeding Israel's $3.18 billion that year. While some figures are still considered "partial," total U.S. aid globally for 2022 currently adds up to more than $60 billion, a level not seen since 1951.

On Monday, Army Secretary Christine Wormuth told reporters additional funds from Congress would be necessary to aid both Israel and Ukraine simultaneously. Meanwhile, the House of Representatives is essentially paralyzed until it selects a new Speaker of the House following Kevin McCarthy's ouster.

Almost all U.S. aid to Israel recently has been military aid rather than economic aid, in the form of Foreign Military Financing grants – U.S. grants and loans to Israel for acquiring U.S. military equipment and services. Israel is typically allowed first access in the region to U.S. defense technology to stay ahead of neighboring militaries, a concept summarized as a "qualitative military edge" by the Congressional Research Service in a report on foreign aid to the country.

The CRS estimates that U.S. military aid reflects 16% of Israel's total defense budget. The non-partisan data center, USA Facts, points out those totals don't include funds for Israel's missile defense systems, which to date have amounted to about $10 billion more in U.S. contributions, according to the CRS report.

The Israel Defense Forces credits one such missile defense system, the Iron Dome, for intercepting 90% of missiles fired into its territory in 2021, but Saturday's attack saw hundreds of missiles rapidly fired, which may have overwhelmed the system. The Iron Dome, which focuses on short-range aerial attacks, was originally developed by Israel's Rafael Advanced Defense

Systems but since 2014 has been co-produced with the United States through a partnership with Raytheon, according to the CRS.

The two companies also developed David's Sling together, a system to counter "long-range rockets and slower-flying cruise missiles," and in 2020 teamed up in a joint venture, Raytheon Rafael Area Protection Systems. Israel Aerospace Industries and Boeing form another U.S.-Israel missile defense partnership, together developing the Arrow systems which cover short-range (Arrow), long-range (Arrow II) and high-altitude (Arrow III) aerial attacks.

Israel's military expenditures are significant when compared to its gross domestic product. In 2022, Israel spent 4.5% of its GDP on its military, according to the World Bank, almost double the global average, and tying other nations at No. 8 for highest military spending when compared as a ratio to GDP. Israel saw that rate peak at 30.5% in 1975, but it has slowly been descending since. For comparison, Ukraine saw the highest share in 2022, with more than one-third (33.5%) of its GDP associated with military expenditures in its ongoing defense against Russia.

Due to its compulsory service at the age of 18 – which requires conscripted men to serve for at least 32 months and conscripted women to serve at least 24 months – Israel has a larger portion of its "economically active population" in the armed forces compared to other countries. At 4.4% in 2020, Israel was well above the global average of 0.8%, tying other nations at No. 6 for the highest share of citizens in the military.

Having to prepare for regular attacks may lead Israelis to take terrorism more seriously compared to others. Earlier this year, as part of the survey that drives the Best Countries rankings, respondents were asked to what extent they agreed or disagreed with the statement "Terrorism is the most important global issue to solve." Among Israeli survey takers, 44% strongly agreed with the statement, and 83.5% agreed to any extent. Meanwhile, the global response saw 30% agreeing strongly and 79.5% agreeing to any extent.

* Dollar amounts sourced from ForeignAssistance.gov are adjusted for inflation, and expressed in constant 2021 dollars as reported by USAID.

Missile defense funding as reported by the Congressional Research Service is expressed in current dollars.

Source: https://www.usnews.com/news/best-countries/articles/2023-10-10/how-much-aid-does-the-u-s-give-to-israel

The Biden administration on Friday laid out the details of a $105 billion national security package that includes military and humanitarian assistance for the conflicts in Ukraine and Israel.

The supplemental request would provide security support to Israel, bolster Israeli efforts to secure the release of hostages and extend humanitarian aid to civilians affected by the war in Israel and Gaza, according to a White House fact sheet.

It would also provide training, equipment and weapons to help Ukraine defend itself against Russia's invasion and to recapture its territory, as well as to protect Ukrainians from Russian aggression, the fact sheet said.

The package would also include additional funds to support US-Mexico border security, including more patrol agents, machines to detect fentanyl, asylum officers and immigration judge teams. Plus, it would provide funding to strengthen security in the Indo-Pacific region, including Taiwan.

Biden makes the case for wartime aid to Israel and Ukraine in primetime address

The funding request, which President Joe Biden pushed for in a prime-time Oval Office address to the nation Thursday, faces an uphill battle in Congress. House Republicans are still struggling to unite behind a speaker to lead their conference, and until one is elected, the national security package will remain in limbo.

Also, support for Ukraine among the public and certain lawmakers has decreased as the war passes its 600th day. The Biden administration's prior request for $24 billion in Ukraine aid was not included in a stopgap government funding measure Congress approved in late September.

Here's what's in the package, according to the White House:

$61.4 billion in aid for Ukraine

- $30 billion for the Defense Department for equipment for Ukraine and the replenishment of US stocks. So far, the US has provided Ukraine with air defense systems, munitions, small arms and ground maneuver units, among other weapons and equipment.

- $14.4 billion for continued military, intelligence and other defense support. This includes investments in the defense industrial base, transportation costs of US personnel and equipment, and continuing an enhanced US troop presence in Europe, among other activities.

- $16.3 billion for economic, security and operational assistance. It includes direct budget support to Ukraine to help it provide critical services to its people and sustain its economy, as well as investments in infrastructure, civilian law enforcement and getting rid of mines.

- $481 million to support Ukrainians arriving in the US through the Uniting for Ukraine program.

- $149 million for the National Nuclear Security Administration for nuclear/radiological incident response and capacity building in case of emergencies as part of general contingency planning.

$14.3 billion in aid for Israel

- $10.6 billion for assistance through the Defense Department, including air and missile defense support, industrial base investments and replenishment of US stocks being drawn down to support Israel.

- The aid aims to bolster Israel's air and missile defense system readiness and support its procurement of Iron Dome and David's Sling missile defense systems and components, as well as the development of the Iron Beam.

- $3.7 billion for the State Department to strengthen Israel's military and enhance US Embassy security.

$10 billion for humanitarian assistance

- $9.15 billion for aid for Ukraine, Israel, Gaza and other humanitarian needs. It includes support for Palestinian refugees in the West Bank and surrounding areas.

- $850 million for migration and refugee assistance at the US-Mexico border.

$7.4 billion for Taiwan and the Indo-Pacific region

- The security assistance aims to bolster deterrence and to support allies facing increasing assertiveness from China and transitioning off Russian military equipment.

- $2 billion for foreign military financing.

- $3.4 billion for the submarine industrial base. It would fund improvements at the Navy's four public shipyards and increase submarine availability.

- $2 billion for the Treasury Department to provide a "credible alternative to coercive financing" and to catalyze billions from other donors through the US-led World Bank. The administration is seeking to offer options other than China's "coercive and unsustainable financing for developing countries."

$13.6 billion to address security at the US-Mexico border

- $6.4 billion for border operations, including additional temporary holding facilities, DNA collection at the border and support for eligible arrivals and unaccompanied children.

- $3.1 billion for an additional 1,300 Border Patrol agents, 1,600 asylum officers, processing personnel and 375 immigration judge teams.

- $1.4 billion for state and local support for temporary shelter, food and other services for migrants recently released from Department of Homeland Security custody.

- $1.2 billion to counter fentanyl, including inspection system deployment, additional Customs and Border Protection officers, and testing and tracing activities.

- $1.4 billion for migration needs to support Safe Mobility Offices, for host communities and legal pathways in the region, for foreign government repatriation operations and to combat human trafficking and smuggling in the Western Hemisphere.

- $100 million for child labor investigations and enforcement, particularly to protect migrant children entering the US through the southern border.

Source: https://edition.cnn.com/2023/10/20/politics/us-israel-ukraine-aid-package/index.html

TRANSPARENCY AND ACCOUNTABILITY IN GOVERNMENT SPENDING

Transparency and accountability in government spending are essential principles of good governance that help ensure that public funds are used efficiently, effectively, and for the benefit of citizens. These principles promote trust in government institutions and foster responsible fiscal management. Here's a closer look at transparency and accountability in government spending:

1. Transparency:

Open Budgeting: Governments should make their budgetary processes transparent by providing detailed information about revenue sources, allocations, and expenditures. This information should be readily accessible to the public.

Financial Reporting: Regular financial reports and statements, including audited financial statements, should be published and made available to the public. These reports should offer a comprehensive view of government finances.

Public Procurement: Transparency in government procurement processes helps prevent corruption and waste. Information about procurement contracts, bidding processes, and awarded contracts should be accessible to the public.

Disclosure of Beneficiaries: Governments should disclose the recipients of public funds, such as individuals or organizations receiving subsidies, grants, or contracts, to ensure fairness and accountability.

Open Data Initiatives: Some governments have launched open data initiatives, making government financial data available in machine-readable formats for easy analysis by researchers, journalists, and the public.

2. Accountability:

Auditing: Independent auditing agencies or bodies should conduct regular financial and performance audits of government agencies and programs. These audits help identify mismanagement, fraud, or inefficiency in spending.

Oversight and Checks: Legislative bodies, such as parliaments or congresses, play a crucial role in holding governments accountable. They review budgets, approve expenditures, and conduct investigations when necessary.

Accountability Mechanisms: Governments can establish mechanisms that allow citizens to report misuse of funds, such as hotlines, whistleblower protections, or online reporting platforms.

Legal Framework: Strong legal frameworks and anti-corruption laws should be in place to penalize individuals or entities involved in corrupt practices related to government spending.

Civil Society Engagement: Civil society organizations, including non-governmental organizations (NGOs) and watchdog groups, can play a critical role in monitoring government spending and advocating for transparency and accountability.

3. Benefits of Transparency and Accountability:

Preventing Corruption: Transparency and accountability measures help identify and prevent corrupt practices, ensuring that public funds are used for their intended purposes.

Enhancing Efficiency: When governments know that their spending decisions will be subject to scrutiny, they are more likely to make efficient and cost-effective choices.

Promoting Trust: Transparency and accountability build trust between citizens and their government, which is essential for social cohesion and political stability.

Effective Resource Allocation: Access to detailed financial data allows policymakers to allocate resources more effectively, prioritizing areas of greatest need.

Citizen Empowerment: When citizens have access to information about government spending, they can engage in informed discussions, advocacy, and oversight, holding their leaders accountable.

Challenges:

Implementing transparency and accountability measures can face resistance from those who benefit from opaque practices.

In some countries, weak institutions, corruption, and lack of political will may hinder efforts to promote transparency and accountability.

Balancing transparency with privacy concerns, particularly when disclosing personal data related to social programs, is an ongoing challenge.

In conclusion, transparency and accountability in government spending are crucial for good governance, fiscal responsibility, and trust in public institutions. Governments, civil society organizations, and citizens should work together to ensure that public funds are used wisely and for the benefit of society as a whole.

CURRENCY DEVALUATION AND LOSS OF PURCHASING POWER

Definition of Currency Devaluation:

Currency devaluation occurs when a government or central bank decides to reduce the value of its currency in relation to other currencies. This is typically done by the government or central bank through monetary policy measures, like when they decide to increase or reduce during certain periods of time their interest rates.

Reasons for Currency Devaluation, Governments may devalue their currency for several reasons:

Export Competitiveness: Devaluation can make a country's exports cheaper in foreign markets, thereby boosting export competitiveness and increasing export volumes. This can help stimulate economic growth by spurring demand for domestically produced goods and services.

Trade Imbalance: Devaluation can also help correct trade imbalances by making imports more expensive and exports more attractive. If a country has a persistent trade deficit (i.e., it imports more than it exports), devaluation can help reduce the deficit by making imports relatively more expensive and exports relatively cheaper.

External Debt: Devaluation can make it easier for a country to service its external debt denominated in foreign currency. Since devaluation makes the country's currency weaker, it reduces the real value of the debt burden in domestic currency terms.

Impact on Purchasing Power:

Currency devaluation can lead to a loss of purchasing power for consumers and businesses within the country. When a currency is devalued, imported goods and services become more expensive, leading to higher prices for imported goods. This can result in inflationary pressures and erode the real incomes of consumers, as their money buys fewer goods and services.

Factors Contributing to Currency Devaluation:

Several factors can contribute to currency devaluation, including:

Inflation Differentials: Persistent inflationary pressures in a country relative to its trading partners can erode the value of its currency and lead to devaluation.

Current Account Deficits: Countries with large and persistent current account deficits may experience pressure on their currency due to the need to finance the deficit through borrowing or selling assets to foreigners.

Speculative Attacks: Speculators may engage in speculative attacks against a currency if they believe it is overvalued or if they anticipate a devaluation. This can put pressure on the currency and force authorities to devalue.

Market Sentiment: Market sentiment and investor confidence can also influence currency values. Negative sentiment or loss of confidence in a country's economic fundamentals can lead to currency depreciation.

Government Intervention:

In some cases, governments may intervene directly in the foreign exchange market to devalue their currency. This can involve selling the country's currency in exchange for foreign currency reserves, thereby increasing the supply of the domestic currency and driving down its value.

In summary, currency devaluation refers to a deliberate reduction in the value of a country's currency relative to other currencies. It can lead to a loss of purchasing power for consumers and businesses and has implications for inflation, trade competitiveness, and external debt management. Devaluation is influenced by various factors, including economic fundamentals, market sentiment, and government policies.

HOW TAX LAWS INFLUENCE INFLATION?

Tax laws can have a significant influence on inflation, although their impact is indirect and often complex. Here's how tax laws can affect inflation:

Consumer Spending and Demand:

Tax laws that influence consumer income, such as income tax rates, can impact the amount of disposable income individuals have available for spending. When income taxes are reduced or tax credits are provided, people often have more money to spend, which can lead to increased consumer demand.

Increased consumer demand, if not matched by a corresponding increase in the supply of goods and services, can put upward pressure on prices, contributing to inflation.

Business Investment and Supply:

Tax policies can influence business decisions regarding investment, production, and hiring. For example, tax incentives for businesses to invest in new equipment or hire more workers can stimulate economic growth.

Conversely, high corporate taxes or taxes on capital gains may discourage investment and business expansion. This can lead to supply bottlenecks, where the supply of goods and services lags behind demand, potentially driving up prices.

Cost-Push Inflation:

Tax laws can also affect costs for businesses. When taxes increase on factors of production, such as labor or raw materials, these higher costs can be passed on to consumers in the form of higher prices for goods and services.

For example, an increase in payroll taxes or tariffs can lead to cost-push inflation if businesses choose to offset those increased costs by raising prices.

Fiscal Policy and Government Spending:

Tax laws are intertwined with government spending policies. When governments run deficits and finance them through borrowing or printing money (monetary expansion), this can increase the money supply, which is a key driver of inflation.

Tax cuts, without corresponding reductions in government spending, can contribute to deficits and inflationary pressures if not offset by other factors.

Inflation Expectations:

Tax laws can influence inflation expectations. When people anticipate future inflation due to expansionary fiscal policies, they may adjust their behavior accordingly. This can lead to wage-price spirals, where workers demand higher wages to keep up with expected price increases, further fueling inflation.

Interest Rates and Monetary Policy:

The interaction between tax laws and central bank policies is crucial. When fiscal policies (tax and spending) are expansionary, central banks may respond by raising interest rates to counter inflationary pressures.

Higher interest rates can impact borrowing costs for businesses and consumers, potentially reducing spending and investment, which can help moderate inflation.

It's important to note that the relationship between tax laws and inflation is not straightforward. Other factors, such as global economic conditions, supply shocks (like energy price fluctuations), and expectations about future inflation, also play significant roles in determining inflation rates.

Governments and central banks typically monitor these complex interactions closely to achieve a balance between economic growth and price stability. The impact of tax laws on inflation is just one element in the broader economic policy landscape, and policymakers must consider multiple factors when making decisions about taxation and fiscal policy.

STRATEGIES FOR MITIGATING INFLATIONARY PRESSURE

Mitigating inflationary pressure is a key goal for governments and central banks to maintain price stability and economic growth. When inflation becomes a concern, policymakers can implement various strategies to address it. Here are some common strategies for mitigating inflationary pressure:

Monetary Policy:

Central banks can use monetary policy tools to control inflation. The most common tool is adjusting the policy interest rate, such as the federal funds rate in the United States.

When inflation is rising, central banks can raise interest rates to make borrowing more expensive. Higher interest rates can reduce consumer spending and business investment, which can help cool down the economy and lower inflation.

Open Market Operations:

Central banks can engage in open market operations by buying or selling government securities in the open market. When central banks sell securities, they withdraw money from the banking system, reducing the money supply and curbing inflationary pressures.

Reserve Requirements:

Central banks can adjust the reserve requirements for banks. Raising reserve requirements means banks must hold more of their deposits in reserves, which reduces the amount of money available for lending and can help slow down economic activity and inflation.

Exchange Rate Policy:

A country's exchange rate policy can influence inflation. A stronger currency can make imported goods cheaper, putting downward pressure on domestic prices. Central banks may intervene in currency markets to influence exchange rates.

Fiscal Policy:

Governments can use fiscal policy, which involves changes in government spending and taxation, to counter inflation. Reducing government spending or increasing taxes can reduce demand in the economy and lower inflationary pressures.

Supply-Side Policies:

Supply-side policies focus on increasing the productive capacity of the economy. Investments in infrastructure, technology, and education can improve productivity, which may help alleviate inflationary pressures by expanding the supply of goods and services.

Wage and Price Controls:

In extreme cases, governments may impose wage and price controls to directly limit the increase in wages and prices. However, this approach is often seen as a last resort due to its potential negative economic consequences.

Communication and Transparency:

Central banks and governments can use effective communication to manage inflation expectations. Clear and transparent communication about monetary and fiscal policies can influence how businesses and consumers plan for the future.

Global Coordination:

In a globalized economy, inflation can be influenced by global factors, such as commodity prices and international supply chains. International coordination among central banks and governments can help address inflationary pressures collectively.

Inflation Targeting:

Many central banks use inflation targeting as a framework for monetary policy. They set explicit inflation targets and adjust their policies to achieve these targets. This approach provides a clear signal to the public about the central bank's commitment to price stability.

It's important to note that the effectiveness of these strategies depends on the specific economic conditions and the nature of the inflationary pressures. Policymakers often need to carefully assess the root causes of inflation and tailor their strategies accordingly. Additionally, the timing and magnitude of policy actions are critical to achieving the desired outcome of mitigating inflation while sustaining economic growth.

Shifting from Taxation to Social Investment:

Shifting from a heavy reliance on taxation to social investment is a significant policy shift that aims to promote economic growth, reduce income inequality, and enhance the overall well-being of a society. This transition involves reallocating government resources from traditional tax collection to targeted investments in education, healthcare, infrastructure, and social programs. Here are some key aspects and considerations for making this transition:

1. Rationale for the Shift:

The rationale behind shifting from taxation to social investment is based on the belief that targeted investments in human capital, infrastructure, and social services can lead to long-term economic growth and improved societal outcomes.

By investing in areas like education and healthcare, governments can potentially reduce the need for costly social safety nets, enhance workforce productivity, and create a healthier and more educated population.

2. Funding Mechanisms:

To finance social investments, governments may need to explore alternative sources of revenue, such as:

Public-Private Partnerships (PPPs): Collaborations with private sector entities to fund and manage infrastructure projects.

Sovereign Wealth Funds: Investment funds funded by government surpluses or income from natural resources.

Impact Bonds: Financial instruments that pay investors a return based on the success of a social program.

User Fees: Charging fees for certain government services or assets, such as tolls for road usage or tuition for higher education.

3. Evaluating Returns on Investment:

Governments must rigorously evaluate the expected returns on social investments. This involves assessing the economic, social, and long-term benefits of each investment.

Cost-benefit analyses, social impact assessments, and ongoing monitoring and evaluation mechanisms are essential tools for ensuring that investments are effective and efficient.

4. Prioritizing Key Sectors:

Governments should identify and prioritize key sectors for social investment based on the country's specific needs and circumstances. Common areas of focus include:

Education: Investments in quality education from early childhood to higher education.

Healthcare: Expanding access to quality healthcare services and preventive measures.

Infrastructure: Building and maintaining critical infrastructure, such as transportation networks, water supply, and energy systems.

Social Safety Nets: Strengthening programs to support vulnerable populations.

5. Balancing Fiscal Responsibility:

It is crucial to maintain fiscal responsibility during the transition. Governments must ensure that social investments do not lead to unsustainable levels of public debt.

Prudent fiscal management, including deficit control and debt sustainability analysis, is essential.

6. Political and Public Support:

Shifting from taxation to social investment may require broad political consensus and public support. Transparency, communication, and engagement with various stakeholders are vital in garnering backing for these changes.

7. Adaptation and Flexibility:

Governments should be prepared to adapt and adjust their strategies as circumstances change. Flexibility and the ability to respond to economic and social shifts are key to the success of such a transition.

8. Learning from Best Practices:

Governments can learn from other countries that have successfully implemented similar shifts toward social investment. Understanding best practices and lessons learned can help inform policy decisions.

Shifting from taxation to social investment is a complex process that requires careful planning, sound economic analysis, and effective governance. When executed thoughtfully, it has the potential to enhance the long-term well-being and prosperity of a nation.

Universal Basic Income (UBI) and Alternatives:

Universal Basic Income (UBI) is a policy proposal that has gained attention as a means to address income inequality and provide financial security to all citizens. It involves giving every eligible individual a regular, unconditional cash payment from the government. While UBI is one approach, there are also alternative policies and strategies to achieve similar goals of reducing poverty and ensuring economic stability. Here, we'll explore UBI and some of its alternatives:

Definition: UBI is a regular cash payment provided by the government to all eligible residents, regardless of their income or employment status. It is typically designed to cover basic living expenses.

Key Features:

Unconditional: UBI is provided without means-testing, work requirements, or restrictions on how the money is spent.

Regular: Payments are made on a regular basis, such as monthly or annually.

Universal: Every eligible resident, including the wealthy, receives the payment.

Potential Benefits:

Poverty Reduction: UBI can reduce poverty rates and provide a financial safety net for all citizens.

Simplified Welfare System: UBI can simplify and replace complex welfare programs.

Economic Stimulus: UBI can boost consumer spending and stimulate economic growth.

Challenges:

Cost: Implementing UBI on a large scale can be costly and may require significant tax increases.

Inflation Concerns: Critics worry that UBI could lead to inflation if not properly financed.

Work Incentives: Some argue that unconditional cash payments may discourage work.

Alternative Policies and Strategies:

Negative Income Tax (NIT):

NIT is a tax policy that provides financial support to individuals or families with incomes below a certain threshold. It is designed to ensure that those with low or no income receive financial assistance through the tax system. NIT provides more substantial support to those with lower incomes and tapers off as income increases.

Targeted Cash Transfers:

Governments can provide cash transfers to specific groups or individuals in need, such as low-income families, single parents, or the unemployed. These targeted programs focus on addressing specific challenges within the population.

Conditional Cash Transfers (CCT):

CCT programs provide cash assistance to individuals or families under the condition that they meet certain criteria, such as sending their children to school or accessing healthcare services. CCTs aim to address both short-term needs and long-term human capital development.

Job Guarantee Programs:

Job guarantee programs provide government-funded employment opportunities to individuals who are willing and able to work. These programs focus on addressing unemployment and underemployment by offering a job with a decent wage and benefits.

Minimum Wage Adjustments:

Increasing the minimum wage to a living wage can help ensure that individuals who work receive an income sufficient to cover their basic needs without the need for additional cash transfers.

Social Services Expansion:

Expanding access to affordable healthcare, education, and housing can directly improve the well-being of citizens by reducing the cost burdens in these areas.

Progressive Taxation:

Implementing a more progressive tax system with higher rates for the wealthy can help redistribute wealth and fund targeted poverty reduction programs.

Basic Services Provision:

Ensuring access to essential public services like healthcare, education, and clean water can alleviate the financial burden on individuals and families.

The choice between UBI and alternative policies often depends on a country's specific goals, economic context, and political priorities. Some countries may adopt a combination of these approaches to address poverty, income inequality, and economic stability effectively. Policymakers consider the costs, administrative feasibility, and potential impact on work incentives when designing and implementing these policies.

The Role of Philanthropy and Public-Private Partnerships

Philanthropy and public-private partnerships (PPPs) play essential roles in addressing societal challenges, promoting social welfare, and advancing economic development. These mechanisms leverage the resources, expertise, and innovation of both the public and private sectors to achieve shared goals. Here's an overview of the roles of philanthropy and PPPs:

Role of Philanthropy:

-Charitable Giving: Philanthropy involves individuals, foundations, corporations, and other entities voluntarily donating money, assets, or resources to support various causes and organizations. This financial support can help address pressing social issues, such as poverty, education, healthcare, and environmental conservation.

-Filling Funding Gaps: Philanthropy can fill funding gaps that government programs or traditional financing mechanisms may not cover. Philanthropic organizations often target underserved or marginalized communities and fund innovative projects.

-Risk-Taking and Innovation: Philanthropy allows for experimentation and risk-taking in addressing complex societal challenges. Foundations and philanthropic donors can support pilot projects, research, and unconventional approaches that government agencies may be hesitant to undertake.

-Advocacy and Policy Influence: Philanthropic organizations often engage in advocacy and policy efforts to influence public policy, raise awareness, and shape discussions on critical issues. They can serve as independent voices advocating for change.

-Catalyzing Social Change: Philanthropy can be a catalyst for social change by supporting organizations that work on systemic issues. Examples include initiatives to reduce income inequality, combat diseases, promote education, and protect human rights.

Role of Public-Private Partnerships (PPPs):

-Resource Mobilization: PPPs leverage private sector resources, including financial capital, technology, and expertise, to complement public sector investments in various projects and initiatives. This shared financial burden can help fund infrastructure development, healthcare services, and education programs.

-Efficiency and Expertise: Private sector partners often bring efficiency, innovation, and specialized knowledge to PPP projects. This can lead to more cost-effective service delivery, improved project management, and enhanced outcomes.

-Risk Sharing: PPPs distribute risks between public and private entities. Private partners may take on some of the project risks, such as construction or operational risks, which can protect taxpayers and incentivize efficient project delivery.

-Innovation and Technology Transfer: Collaboration with the private sector can facilitate the transfer of cutting-edge technologies and best practices to the public sector. This can lead to improvements in areas like healthcare, renewable energy, and transportation.

-Accountability and Performance Metrics: PPPs often establish clear performance metrics and accountability mechanisms for private partners. These agreements help ensure that projects are delivered on time, on budget, and according to specified quality standards.

-Scale and Reach: PPPs can expand the scale and reach of public services. For example, partnerships with telecommunications companies have extended access to mobile banking and digital services in remote areas.

-Sustainable Development: PPPs can support sustainable development goals by addressing environmental concerns, promoting responsible business practices, and aligning projects with long-term sustainability objectives.

While both philanthropy and PPPs have their distinct roles and contributions, they can also intersect in various ways. For example, philanthropic organizations may provide initial seed funding for PPP projects, and private sector entities may engage in philanthropic activities as part of their corporate social responsibility efforts.

Ultimately, both philanthropy and PPPs are valuable tools for addressing complex societal challenges, fostering innovation, and achieving positive social and economic outcomes. Collaboration between the public and private sectors, alongside philanthropic support, can lead to more holistic and effective approaches to pressing global issues.

DO YOU HAVE ENOUGH NON-DEBT MONEY?

Recently Ray Dalyo (Founder, CIO Mentor, and Member of the Bridgewater Board) wrote an article via LinkedIn, which we find interesting on the issue about fiat currency when governments print money and make it circulate as debt. We wanted to share this insight with you to analyze better or our new macroeconomic theory:

--

Good money is both a good medium of exchange and a good store hold of wealth that is widely accepted around the world. The most globally recognized and accepted monies are the dollar, to a lesser extent the euro, to a much lesser extent the yen, and to an even lesser extent the Chinese Renminbi. These monies are held in debt assets—i.e., they are debt-backed money—i.e., **currency = debt.** In other words, when you hold these monies, you are holding debt liabilities, which are promises to deliver you money.

History and logic show that when there are big risks that the debts will either 1) not be paid back or 2) be paid back with money of depreciated value, the debt and the money become unattractive. Since debts are promises to pay money, when a government has too much debt to be paid, its central bank is likely to print money. This prevents a big debt squeeze from happening by devaluing the money (i.e., inflation).

Gold, on the other hand, is a non-debt-backed form of money. It's like cash, except unlike cash and bonds, which are devalued by risks of default or inflation, gold is supported by risks of debt defaults and inflation. It is held by central banks and other investors for this reason. In fact, gold is the third-most-held reserve currency by central banks, more so than the Yen or Renminbi. Cryptocurrencies are also non-debt monies. I don't know of any other types of non-debt monies, though some people might argue that gems and art act similarly because they are non-debt, portable, and widely accepted storeholds of wealth.

When the financial system is working well—which is when there aren't debt and inflation crises and the borrower-debtor governments printing debt-backed monies are meeting their obligations and paying their interest without printing and devaluing money—debt assets and other financial assets are good assets to hold; on the other hand, when the reverse is the case, gold is a good asset to own. That's the main reason that gold is a good diversifier and why I have some in my portfolio.

PS: To be clear, I am trying to share my thoughts with you about investments but not give investment advice. So I am not recommending that you buy gold. In my communications with you, I am trying to convey to you how the markets work, explain what I think you should be aware of, and give some strategic investment thinking.

Disclosures

Bridgewater Daily Observations is prepared by and is the property of Bridgewater Associates, LP and is circulated for informational and educational purposes only. There is no consideration given to the specific investment needs, objectives, or tolerances of any of the recipients. Additionally, Bridgewater's actual investment positions may, and often will, vary from its conclusions discussed herein based on any number of factors, such as client investment restrictions, portfolio rebalancing and transactions costs, among others. Recipients should consult their own advisors, including tax advisors, before making any investment decision. This material is for informational and educational purposes only and is not an offer to sell or the solicitation of an offer to buy the securities or other instruments mentioned. Any such offering will be made pursuant to a definitive offering memorandum. This material does not constitute a personal recommendation or take into account the particular investment objectives, financial situations, or needs of individual investors which are necessary considerations before making any investment decision. Investors should consider whether any advice or recommendation in this research is suitable for their particular circumstances and, where appropriate, seek professional advice, including legal, tax, accounting, investment, or other advice.

--

GOVERNMENT FEES Vs TAXES

Government fees and taxes are both forms of government revenue, but they differ in their characteristics, purposes, and how they are imposed. Here are the key differences between government fees and taxes:

Government Fees:

Purpose: Government fees are charges imposed by the government for specific services, licenses, or regulatory activities. They are often intended to cover the cost of providing a particular service or regulating a specific industry or activity.

Voluntary Nature: Fees are generally considered voluntary in the sense that they are incurred by individuals or businesses that choose to use a government service or engage in an activity that requires regulation.

Quid Pro Quo: There is often a direct relationship between the fee paid and the service received or the regulatory oversight provided. The fee payer expects a benefit or service in return for the payment.

Examples: Common examples of government fees include driver's license fees, passport fees, vehicle registration fees, building permit fees, and tuition fees at public universities.

Regulatory Purpose: Some fees are imposed as a regulatory tool to control certain activities. For example, application fees for professional licenses help ensure that only qualified individuals are allowed to practice in specific fields.

Government Taxes:

Purpose: Taxes are compulsory financial charges imposed by the government on individuals, businesses, and other entities to raise revenue for public expenditures, such as infrastructure, healthcare, education, defense, and social services.

Mandatory Nature: Taxes are mandatory, meaning that individuals and businesses are legally required to pay them based on their income, property, or consumption, regardless of whether they use specific government services.

Redistribution: Taxes are often used to redistribute wealth and income within society. Progressive tax systems, for example, impose higher tax rates on those with higher incomes to support social programs and reduce income inequality.

General Funds: Tax revenues typically go into the government's general funds and are used to finance a wide range of public services and functions.

Examples: Common types of taxes include income taxes, property taxes, sales taxes, corporate taxes, and payroll taxes.

Key Differences:

Purpose: Fees are intended to cover the cost of specific services or regulation, while taxes are primarily aimed at raising general revenue for the government.

Voluntary vs. Mandatory: Fees are incurred voluntarily by individuals or businesses that use specific services or engage in regulated activities, whereas taxes are mandatory and apply to a broader range of economic activities and income.

Direct vs. Indirect Relationship: Fees have a direct quid pro quo relationship with the services provided, while taxes do not have a direct one-to-one relationship between the payment and specific government services.

Usage of Revenue: Fee revenues are often earmarked for the particular service or regulation they support, while tax revenues generally go into the government's general funds for a wide range of public spending.

In summary, government fees are charges for specific services or regulation with a voluntary aspect, while taxes are compulsory payments that go into general government revenue for broader public purposes. Both play important roles in government finance, but they serve different functions and have distinct characteristics.

THE NO-TAXES THEORY AND HOW TO MAKE IT WORK:

Let's take a look at governments once they are about to start a new year, what is it that they do first? They have to budget and plan ahead based on what they want to execute and the resources required to function and achieve results.

This budget comes into many forms and wide areas of interest, that will result as beneficial to the general public in one city, state or country.

How much will we need for public spending, to pay all government employees?

How much are we investing into various areas like education, healthcare programs, military, police force, nature conservation, infrastructure construction, homes, schools, universities, airports, roads, railroads, ports, energy, technology adoption and development, communications, sports, music, art, entertainment, etc. All of this areas should have a positive impact in everybody's lives.

Imagine for a moment that there is no restriction on the total needed or required as a budget variable, call it income, savings or just funds available to execute governments term plan. In this case we talk about the own national currency.

Then again the government owns the printing machine, the central bank that more and more do not print paper money nowadays as everything has become digital mostly with the cell phone in our hands. It means that they can "print" by just adding numbers 1 and 0 into their computers, software and data base. They create public debt, bonds that place it or sell into the market at certain interest rates and maturity depending on the actual situation of the economy.

There is a change or a new trend for some years now and specially after Covid19 pandemic, everything to become digital, given that it is less expensive, less bureaucracy, more secure, fast, reliable and open. This is why Blockchain technology and Crypto space are here to stay with more or less two trillion market cap.

This industry has been evolving fast, alongside with robotics and now AI (Artificial Intelligence). Many countries and companies are shifting, like El Salvador in Central America, they now accept Bitcoin (BTC) as legal tender, MacDonalds, Tesla, Honda, AMC theaters, Starbucks, Uber, Home Depot and many other within different industries are accepting it, including some banks themselves.

There is a global competition on payment methods, tools and options in every country, basically given that the USD and any other currency has been losing ground against inflation and you cannot buy the same with 10 USD 7 years ago, than today with the same USD 10. We have shifted to USD worldwide currency reserve status and national currencies to micro economies. For example, you can go to the grocery store and pay with points that have been accumulated from previous purchases, you can buy airline tickets with miles that you accumulated in previous trips or even with the supermarket points you can buy air tickets also. Nowadays there are many options to solve our daily purchase and transactional needs highly influenced by technology growth.

Positive Economic Outcomes from a no tax law:

Increased Disposable Income: With no taxes on income, individuals and corporations would have more disposable income. This could stimulate consumer spending, boost investment, and encourage economic activity that will lead to closing the inequality gap and wealth distribution.

Many companies file for bankruptcy just because they are not competitive on that tax % structure that affects their business.

Reduced price pressure on goods: There are many different types of taxes on goods, from 4% to 14%, 19%, 25%, depending on the country and the type of goods sold. This will lead to lower prices, competitiveness and less inflationary outcomes.

Enhanced Business Investment: Corporations might allocate a more significant portion of their profits to business expansion, research and development, and innovation. Some conditions for this to happen it's that if corporations want to move abroad their profits from the country, there will be a penalty to do that. In this way to ensure profits are reinvested in the country.

But if you look at it from a foreign investor point of view, they come to the country, bring capital, build infrastructure to operate, hire local employees and move the economy. It is already a win-win deal for the country. Even if they don't pay taxes or move the profits out, given the case.

Competitiveness: Lower corporate taxes could make a country more attractive to businesses, potentially leading to increased foreign direct investment and job creation.

Simplified Tax System: Eliminating taxes would simplify the tax system, reducing compliance costs for individuals and businesses.

PRINT WHAT YOU NEED TO SOURCE RATIONAL SOUND PUBLIC PLANNING AND FUNCTIONING > INVEST IN YOUR OWN COUNTRY AND PEOPLE = ECONOMIC GROWTH = SOCIAL BENEFITS AND QUALITY OF LIFE = BETTER FUTURE FOR EVERYBODY.

The other part of the problem is that all money needed by governments when printed it is called public debt, which makes no sense as this money goes back to the same people in the country in many beneficial ways, education, healthcare, infrastructure, defense, laws, technology, sports, recreation, leisure and many other aspects that make part of a modern society. So paying interest seems like paying double on what you give to the nation or people.

Normally the governments issue bonds at some interest rate and maturity to raise funds, but this interest has to be paid and where is that money coming from? Tax payers money.

We have to think as one entity, one country and everything we do will benefit us all.

Governments are there to serve people and to give, not to take away. If we trust our governments, our laws, our economy structure, our people and our currency, to put in place the no tax theory will be a lot easier. Think of it as on a balance sheet, we have assets (the first line it is cash available). All this cash will be given to the nation in different ways, like infrastructure, roads, education, defense, technology, etc. In this case with the goal to benefit everybody, to make life easier and grow a stronger economy. We will also have to pay our public servants which it is part of the package. People will not have the need to pay any taxes so to compensate interest on loans made by your government, instead companies and people will use this funds to put them back, spend or invest into the economy.

Then again it is good for the government that will not be limited on the resources, interest rates, debt ceilings or liquidity to conduct its investments and sound expenses.

Few exceptions on taxes required:

Policies that will continue have a different approach and will gradually dismount as long as there is international cooperation:

Environmental Impact: Taxes are sometimes used to incentivize environmentally friendly behavior. The elimination of such taxes could hinder efforts to address environmental issues. Here again, it's kind of simple to solve. The government will have enough resources to implement environmental programs to help achieve net zero emissions or fight climate change, these can be run also by private companies. This programs result in economic benefits and in line to the United Nations Sustainable Development Goals. The taxes or fees are to compensate the contamination levels or GHG emissions. By buying credits from environmental, green energy, tech, conservation projects or similar, they can compensate or offset their foot print.

This is a very different concept and it is to help fight climate change that endanger human life civilization and all species on earth.

Taxes on imports

Taxes on imports are commonly known as tariffs or import duties. They are a type of tax imposed by a government on goods and services that are imported into a country. These taxes serve various economic and policy purposes, and their impact can be significant. Here are some key points about taxes on imports:

1. Revenue Generation: One primary purpose of import taxes is to generate revenue for the government. Customs authorities collect tariffs at border crossings or ports of entry, and these revenues can be used to fund government programs and services.

2. Protectionism: Import taxes can also serve as a form of protectionism to shield domestic industries from foreign competition. By imposing tariffs, a country can make imported goods more expensive, thus making domestically produced goods more competitive.

3. Economic Policy Tools: Governments can use import taxes as economic policy tools. For example, they may adjust tariffs to encourage or discourage the importation of specific products. Higher tariffs on certain goods can discourage imports and promote domestic production.

4. Trade Balancing: Import taxes can be used to address trade imbalances. If a country consistently imports more than it exports, it may use tariffs to reduce imports and improve its trade balance.

5. Source of Tension: Tariffs can be a source of tension in international trade relations. Disputes over the imposition of tariffs and accusations of unfair trade practices can lead to trade conflicts between countries.

6. Consumer Impact: Import taxes can increase the cost of imported goods for consumers. This, in turn, can lead to higher prices, reduced consumer choices, and potentially inflationary pressures in the economy.

7. Business Impact: Companies that rely on imported raw materials or components may face increased production costs when import taxes are imposed. This can affect the competitiveness of domestic industries.

8. Trade Agreements: Many countries negotiate trade agreements, such as free trade agreements or customs unions, that reduce or eliminate import taxes on goods traded between member nations. These agreements aim to promote trade and economic cooperation.

9. Classification and Valuation: Import taxes are often based on the classification and valuation of imported goods. Customs authorities use international harmonized codes and customs valuation methods to determine the applicable tariff rates.

10. Non-Tariff Barriers: In addition to tariffs, governments may use non-tariff barriers, such as quotas, licensing requirements, and technical standards, to regulate and restrict imports. These measures can have similar effects on trade as import taxes.

It's important to note that the impact of import taxes depends on various factors, including the specific goods subject to tariffs, the level of tariffs, and the response of trading partners. Trade policy is a complex and evolving area that is influenced by economic, political, and strategic considerations.

Taxes on exports

Taxes on exports, also known as export duties or export tariffs, are government-imposed taxes or levies on goods and services that are sold to foreign markets. These taxes are less common than import tariffs but can be used for various economic and policy purposes. Here are some key points about taxes on exports:

1. **Revenue Generation:** One primary purpose of export taxes is to generate revenue for the government. These revenues can be used to fund public services, infrastructure development, or other government initiatives.

2. **Commodity Exporting Countries:** Some countries that heavily rely on the export of specific commodities, such as oil, minerals, or agricultural products, may impose export taxes to capture a share of the profits generated from the sale of these resources.

3. **Price Stabilization:** Export taxes can be used to stabilize domestic prices for certain goods. By taxing exports, a government can discourage the sale of products abroad, ensuring a sufficient domestic supply and preventing price spikes.

4. **Promoting Domestic Industry:** In some cases, export taxes are used to encourage domestic processing or value addition to raw materials. By taxing raw material exports but not processed products, governments aim to promote local industry and job creation.

5. **Economic Policy Tool:** Export taxes can serve as an economic policy tool. Governments may adjust export tax rates to manage currency exchange rates, trade balances, or the competitiveness of domestic industries.

6. **Source of Revenue for Developing Countries:** Developing countries may rely on export taxes, particularly on natural resources, as a significant source of government revenue. These taxes can help fund essential services and development projects.

7. **Trade Disputes:** Export taxes can be a source of trade disputes when they are perceived as distorting international trade. Exporting countries may challenge the imposition of such taxes through trade negotiations or dispute resolution mechanisms.

8. **Impact on Foreign Buyers:** Export taxes can increase the cost of goods for foreign buyers, making the exported products less competitive in

international markets. This can affect demand for the products and may lead to reduced export volumes.

9. **Unpredictability:** The imposition of export taxes can introduce uncertainty for businesses engaged in international trade. Sudden changes in export tax rates can disrupt trade patterns and affect business planning.

10. **Compliance and Administration:** Like import tariffs, export taxes require customs authorities to administer and collect the tax. This can involve classification, valuation, and documentation procedures.

It's worth noting that export taxes are subject to international trade rules and agreements. Many countries are members of international organizations, such as the World Trade Organization (WTO), which sets rules and guidelines on trade policies, including export taxes. These rules aim to promote fair and predictable trade practices and prevent arbitrary or discriminatory taxation of exports.

So it is not a question of how many trees we have to cut in order to have enough paper available so that a government can run and maintain their investment programs. We are talking about a sound program that will bring benefits to people in the short, mid and long run. It also means that the GDP will increase more by being able to make these investments and not cutting corners on things that are really important or needed. This mostly happens in non-developed countries, they tend to leave aside plans, programs or investments that are truly needed, helpful and useful for the nation, just because a lack of resources.

This seems to me like a mentality, cultural background, education mindset to limit ourselves in what we can do or create altogether as a nation and society.

I see for example in South America there are vast parcels of land, forests with no owner, that they call "no man's land" but indeed it belongs to the government. No one lives there, no production of any type occurs or no development at all. So, the result it is that this land does not account within the country's GDP given its neutral or non-productive status. And the truth is that there's many activities that can be performed in it if given to the right people for development, like conservation projects helping fight climate change, SDG's Sustainable Development Goals, generate income for indigenous communities in forms of Carbon credits or captures, tourism, scientific research, agriculture, cattle ranching, roads, etc.

Impact on Tax Authorities:

If a new no tax law on people or corporations were to be implemented worldwide, it would have significant implications for tax authorities like the Internal Revenue Service (IRS) in the United States and tax agencies globally. Here are some potential consequences and considerations for employees of tax authorities:

1. Reduced Workload:

With no taxes to collect or enforce, tax authorities would have a significantly reduced workload. This would affect various departments within these agencies, including tax collection, audit, compliance, and legal divisions.

2. Downsizing and Restructuring:

The reduction in workload could lead to downsizing and restructuring within tax authorities. Positions related to tax collection and enforcement may become redundant, leading to layoffs or early retirements for some employees.

3. Shift in Responsibilities:

Employees who previously focused on tax collection and enforcement may need to transition to other roles within the government or seek employment in different sectors. This could involve retraining and acquiring new skills.

4. Focus on Other Functions:

Tax authorities often perform functions beyond tax collection, such as data analysis, economic research, and policy development. These functions may continue, albeit with a different focus, even if taxes are eliminated.

5. Impact on Revenue:

Eliminating taxes would have a profound impact on government revenue. Governments would need to find alternative sources of funding to maintain essential services, which could involve new revenue models or funding mechanisms.

6. Transition Period:

Implementing a no-tax law worldwide would likely require a transition period during which tax authorities would need to wind down their existing operations, reassign employees, and adapt to the new economic paradigm.

7. Economic Implications:

The removal of taxes on corporations and individuals could lead to significant changes in economic behavior, investment patterns, and wealth distribution. Governments may need to monitor these changes and adjust their policies accordingly.

8. Legal and Regulatory Functions:

While taxes may be eliminated, governments would still need regulatory and legal frameworks to govern economic activities, contracts, property rights, and more. Employees responsible for these functions would remain essential.

9. Potential New Roles:

In a world without taxes, governments may explore alternative means of revenue generation, such as user fees, natural resource royalties, or public-private partnerships. Employees involved in designing, implementing, and managing these new revenue models would play crucial roles.

10. International Implications:

- Implementing a no-tax law worldwide would require extensive international cooperation and coordination. Tax authorities may continue to participate in global economic governance efforts, albeit with a different focus.

It's important to note that the transition to a tax-free world would be a complex and multifaceted process, and its success would depend on various factors, including political will, economic feasibility, and the ability to maintain essential public services. Additionally, the exact impact on employees of tax authorities would vary depending on the specific legislation, policies, and economic circumstances in each country.

On Judicial and Incarceration systems:

If we assume that sufficient funding will always be available for the judicial and incarceration systems despite the absence of taxes, the implications change significantly. In such a scenario, where alternative funding sources are secure, the impact on the judicial and incarceration systems would be as follows:

1. Increased Focus on Efficiency and Effectiveness:

With a guaranteed budget, the judicial system could place a stronger emphasis on efficiency and effectiveness. This might involve modernizing court processes, reducing case backlogs, and implementing technology-driven improvements.

Also there would not be a need to pursue "tax offenders", releasing this burden from thousands of public employees or even millions around the globe trying to prove that there were felonies made, tax evasion and to put them into trial. It will represent billions and time savings from this scenario.

2. Enhanced Access to Justice:

Adequate funding could lead to improved access to justice for all citizens. Legal aid programs, public defenders, and support services would be well-funded, ensuring that individuals have access to representation and fair treatment in the legal system.

3. Investment in Rehabilitation and Reentry Programs:

In the incarceration system, sufficient funding would allow for greater investments in rehabilitation, education, and vocational training programs for inmates. This could enhance inmates' chances of successful reintegration into society after release.

4. Emphasis on Criminal Justice Reform:

The availability of funding could facilitate broader criminal justice reform efforts, including the exploration of alternatives to incarceration, diversion programs, and restorative justice practices.

5. Improved Conditions in Prisons:

Adequate resources would enable governments to maintain safe and humane conditions in prisons, address overcrowding, and invest in modern facilities.

6. Specialized Courts and Programs:

Specialized courts, such as drug courts, mental health courts, and veterans courts, could receive consistent support, helping individuals with specific needs access appropriate treatment and rehabilitation.

7. Investment in Training and Development:

Judges, prosecutors, public defenders, and law enforcement personnel could receive ongoing training and development, ensuring that they are well-equipped to handle complex legal challenges and cases.

8. Legal Innovation:

A stable funding environment could foster legal innovation, encouraging experimentation with new legal processes, dispute resolution mechanisms, and court technologies to improve the legal system.

9. Reduced Backlogs and Delays:

The availability of resources could lead to a reduction in case backlogs and delays in court proceedings, promoting timely justice delivery.

10. Strengthened Rule of Law:

- A well-funded judicial system can contribute to the maintenance of the rule of law, which is essential for social stability and economic development.

11. Potential for Research and Development:

- Adequate funding could support research and development efforts in the legal and criminal justice fields, leading to the development of best practices and evidence-based policies.

While a hypothetical scenario with guaranteed funding for the judicial and incarceration systems addresses many of the financial challenges, it's important to recognize that other policy and societal factors can influence the effectiveness of these systems. These include legal frameworks, public attitudes, and the broader criminal justice and legal ecosystem. Nevertheless, secure funding would create an environment in which these systems could focus more fully on achieving their core objectives, which include development, justice, rehabilitation, and public safety.

CHAPTER III
WORLD MACROECONOMIC OUTLOOK AND FACTS

2023 UNITED STATES BANKING CRISIS:

Over the course of five days in March 2023, three small- to mid-size U.S. banks failed, triggering a sharp decline in global bank stock prices and swift response by regulators to prevent potential global contagion. Silicon Valley Bank (SVB) failed when a bank run was triggered after it sold its Treasury bond portfolio at a large loss, causing depositor concerns about the bank's liquidity. The bonds had lost significant value as market interest rates rose after the bank had shifted its portfolio to longer-maturity bonds. The bank's clientele was primarily technology companies and wealthy individuals holding large deposits, but balances exceeding $250,000 were not insured by the Federal Deposit Insurance Corporation (FDIC). Silvergate Bank and Signature Bank, both with significant exposure to cryptocurrency, failed in the midst of turbulence in that market.

In response to the bank failures, the three major U.S. federal bank regulators announced in a joint communiqué that extraordinary measures would be taken to ensure that all deposits at Silicon Valley Bank and Signature Bank would be honored. The Federal Reserve established a Bank Term Funding Program (BTFP) to offer loans of up to one year to eligible depository institutions pledging qualifying assets as collateral.

To prevent the situation from affecting more banks, global industry regulators, including the Federal Reserve, the Bank of Canada, Bank of England, Bank of Japan, European Central Bank, and Swiss National Bank intervened to provide extraordinary liquidity.

By March 16, large interbank flows of funds were occurring to shore up bank balance sheets and some analysts were talking of a possibly broader U.S. banking crisis. The Federal Reserve discount window liquidity facility had experienced approximately $150 billion in borrowing from various banks by March 16.

Soon after the bank run at SVB, depositors quickly began withdrawing cash from San Francisco-based First Republic Bank (FRB), which focused on private banking to wealthy clientele. Like SVB, FRB had substantial uninsured deposits exceeding $250,000; such deposits constituted 68% of the bank's total at year-end 2022, declining to 27% by the end of March, as $100 billion in uninsured deposits were withdrawn. Despite a $30 billion capital infusion from a group of major banks in March, FRB continued to destabilize and its stock price plummeted as the FDIC prepared to take it into receivership and find a buyer on April 29. On May 1, the FDIC announced that First Republic had been closed and sold to JPMorgan Chase.

Background:

In the lead-up period, many banks within the United States had invested their reserves in U.S. Treasury securities, which had been paying low interest rates for several years. As the Federal Reserve began raising interest rates in 2022 in response to the 2021–2023 inflation surge, bond prices declined, decreasing the market value of bank capital reserves, causing some banks to incur unrealized losses; to maintain liquidity, Silicon Valley Bank sold its bonds to realize steep losses. Also, several banks gained market exposure to cryptocurrency and cryptocurrency-related firms prior to and during the COVID-19 pandemic; the 2020–2022 cryptocurrency bubble popped in late 2022. In this environment, three such banks failed or were shut down by regulators: The first bank to fail, cryptocurrency-focused Silvergate Bank, announced it would wind down on March 8, 2023 due to losses suffered in its loan portfolio. Two days later, upon announcement of an attempt to raise capital, a bank run occurred at Silicon Valley Bank, causing it to collapse and be seized by regulators that day. Signature Bank, a bank that frequently did business with cryptocurrency firms, was closed by regulators two days later on March 12, with regulators citing systemic risks. The collapses of First Republic Bank, Silicon Valley Bank and Signature Bank were the second-, third- and fourth-largest bank failures in the history of the United States, respectively, smaller only than the collapse of Washington Mutual during the 2007–2008 financial crisis.

In 2019, the Federal Reserve's "Tailoring rules" changed, increasing minimum asset threshold from $50 billion to $100 billion and reduced the number of required stress testing scenarios, allowing banks with under $100 billion to have reduced liquidity standards. Signature Bank and First Republic Bank were under the $100 billion total assets for the Federal Reserve's tailoring rules, allowing the banks to have reduced regulation for liquidity. Some have questioned if First Republic Bank would have had a bank run if there were similar regulation to EU countries in the United States.

Aftermath - Federal response

Bank Term Funding Program

In response to the bank failures of March, the government took extraordinary measures to mitigate fallout across the banking sector. On March 12, Federal Reserve created the Bank Term Funding Program (BTFP), an emergency lending program providing loans of up to one year in length to banks, savings associations, credit unions, and other eligible depository institutions that pledge U.S. Treasuries, agency debt and mortgage-backed securities, and other qualifying assets as collateral. The program is designed to provide liquidity to financial institutions, following the collapse of Silicon Valley Bank and other bank failures, and to reduce the risks associated with current unrealized losses in the U.S. banking system that totaled over $600 billion at the time of the program's launch. Funded through the Deposit Insurance Fund, the program offers loans of up to one year to eligible borrowers who pledge as collateral certain types of securities including U.S. Treasuries, agency debt, and mortgage-backed securities. The collateral will be valued at par instead of open-market value, so a bank can borrow on asset values that have not been impaired by a series of interest rate hikes since 2022. The Federal Reserve also eased conditions at its discount window. The Department of the Treasury will make available up to $25 billion from its Exchange Stabilization Fund as a backstop for the program.

In addition to working with their counterparts at the FDIC and U.S. Treasury to provide liquidity to banks through the BTFP, the Federal Reserve has begun to internally discuss implementing stricter capital reserve and liquidity requirements for banks with between $100 billion and $250 billion in assets on their balance sheets. A review of regulations affecting regional banks has been ongoing since 2022, as Federal Reserve vice chairman Michael Barr and other officials in the Biden Administration had become increasingly concerned about the risk posed to the financial system by the rapidly increasing size of regional banks.

Economic impact

As depositors began to move money en masse from smaller banks to larger banks, on Monday, March 13, shares of regional banks fell.

Following SVB and Signature's collapses, Western Alliance Bancorporation share price fell 47% and PacWest Bancorp was down 21% recovering after their trading was halted. Moody's downgraded its outlook on the U.S. banking system to negative, citing what it described as "rapid deterioration" of the sector's financial footing. It also downgraded the credit ratings of several regional banks, including Western Alliance, First Republic, Intrust Bank, Comerica, UMB Financial Corporation, and Zions Bancorporation. Large declines in regional bank stocks continued after First Republic's failure.

U.S. President Joe Biden made a statement about the first three bank failures on March 13, and asserted that government intervention was not a bailout and that the banking system was stable.

The initial bank failures led to speculation on March 13 that the Federal Reserve could pause or halt rate hikes. Beginning on March 13, traders began modifying their strategies in the expectation that fewer hikes than previously expected will occur.[105] Some financial experts suggested that the BTFP, combined with a recent practice of finding buyers who would cover all deposits, may have effectively removed the FDIC's $250,000 deposit insurance limit. However, Treasury Secretary Janet Yellen clarified that any guarantee beyond that limit would need the approval of the Biden administration and Federal regulators.

The initial three bank failures and resulting pressures on other U.S. regional banks were expected to reduce available financing in the commercial real estate market and further slow commercial property development. The Federal Reserve's discount window liquidity facility saw around $150 billion in borrowing from various banks by March 16, more than 12 times the $12 billion that the BTFP provided. Since the majority of First Republic's long term assets were in municipal bonds, it was unable to make full use of the BTFP as those assets did not qualify as an eligible collateral.

By March 16, large inter-bank flows of funds were occurring to shore up bank balance sheets and numerous analysts were reporting on a more general U.S. banking crisis. Many banks had invested their reserves in U.S. Treasury securities, which had been paying low interest rates. As the Federal Reserve began raising rates in 2022, bond prices declined decreasing the market value of bank capital reserves, leading some banks to sell the bonds at steep losses as yields on new bonds were much higher.

On March 17, President Joe Biden stated that the banking crisis had calmed down, while the New York Times said that the March banking crisis was hanging over the economy and had rekindled fear of recession as business borrowing would become more difficult as many regional and community banks would have to reduce lending.

Late on Sunday, the Federal Reserve and several other central banks announced significant USD liquidity measures in order to calm market turmoil. In a "coordinated action to enhance the provision of liquidity through the standing U.S. dollar swap line arrangements", the U.S. Federal Reserve, the Bank of Canada, Bank of Japan, European Central Bank, and Swiss National Bank joined together to organize daily U.S. dollar swap operations. These swaps had previously been set up to occur on a weekly cadence.

The share price of PacWest had fallen sharply on 3 May after the bank announced that it was 'considering strategic options including a sale'. On 4 May share trading was suspended as the sell-off marked a further 42% loss with other US regional banks, including First Horizon, Metropolitan Bank and Western Alliance, also being affected.

In May 2023, FDIC proposed imposing higher fees on an estimated 113 of the largest banks to cover the costs of bailing out uninsured depositors.

International impact

By 19 March, concerns about the banking sector internationally had increased. That day, Swiss bank UBS Group AG bought its smaller competitor Credit Suisse in an emergency arrangement brokered by the Swiss government. One month before the events in the United States, Credit Suisse had announced its largest annual loss since the 2008 financial crisis, as clients continued withdrawing their cash at a rapid pace; $147 billion had been withdrawn in the fourth quarter of 2022. It also disclosed it had found "material weaknesses" in its financial reporting. Its largest investor, Saudi National Bank, announced on March 15 that it would not provide more support to Credit Suisse. Its share price plunged 25% on the news and UBS stepped in to buy the bank. Axel Lehmann, former chairman of the bank, later sought to blame the American bank failures for triggering Credit Suisse's demise, though other analysts disputed that characterization. The bank had experienced many years of multi-billion dollar losses, scandals, executive turnover and weak business strategy.

Late on Sunday the Federal Reserve and several other central banks announced significant USD liquidity measures in order to calm market turmoil. In a "coordinated action to enhance the provision of liquidity through the standing U.S. dollar swap line arrangements", the U.S. Federal Reserve, the Bank of Canada, Bank of Japan, European Central Bank (ECB) and Swiss National Bank joined together to organize daily U.S. dollar swap operations. These swaps had previously been set up to occur on a weekly cadence.

On 21 March, The Business Times reported that Asian central banks were "unlikely to be greatly influenced by the banking crisis in the United States and Europe", but Australia's central bank governors met and publicly indicated a potential pause in recent rate hikes. ABC News reported that the challenge for central banks is determining if the "banking turmoil close to crashing the real economy, or is inflation still the greater threat." In Japan the three main lenders, Mitsubishi UFJ Financial Group, Sumitomo Mitsui Financial Group and Mizuho Financial Group, lost share value between 10% and 12% due to the market turmoil and their exposure to the bond market. Japan's central bank held a crisis meeting in mid-March while the Topix banks index fell 17%. The fall was led by fears over the SVB collapse and the risks in Japan's regional banking sector, partly because of exposure to US interest rate hikes.

The cost to insure against default on Deutsche Bank debt rose substantially on Friday, 24 March, with the 5-year CDS for the bank's debt rising 70%. The ECB and other European central banks raised interest rates the same day. The European STOXX 600 index fell around 4% with shares in Deutsche Bank down more than 14% at one point, closing the day at a loss of around 8%. The UK's banking index also fell around 3% led by falls of around 6% for both Barclays and Standard Chartered and a 4% drop for NatWest. Shares in other European banks also fell, among them Commerzbank, Austria's Raiffeisen Bank and the French Société Générale. According to the European Commission's Paolo Gentiloni, finance ministers in the Euro zone called on the Commission to close loopholes in Crisis Management and Deposit Insurance (CMDI) provision, starting in the second quarter of 2023.

Chinese banks experienced little negative effect. According to Bloomberg News, almost all of the 166 top performers during the market turmoil were in China. The banking crisis in the U.S. and Europe highlighted the relative stability of the Chinese banking system. While China's recovery from the pandemic remains fragile, inflation there is muted, and the People's Bank of China had adjusted interest rates at a slower pace than Western central banks.

The turbulence in the financial system caused India's central bank to put any further hikes in interest rate on hold on 6 April, with governor Shaktikanta Das saying "it's a pause not a pivot". A 25 basis point increase had been widely expected. Central banks in Australia, Canada and Indonesia also paused any further increases.

While rising interest rates give banks greater returns on customer's loans, the tighter financial conditions meant the sector saw a downturn in equity funding, with the S&P 500 bank index (SPXBK) in April down 14% year to date on expectation of lower quarterly earnings for some US banks. Effects on the secondary market were also expected. On 11 April the International Monetary Fund downgraded its forecast for GDP growth globally in 2023 from 2.9% to 2.8%, saying "Uncertainty is high and the balance of risks has shifted firmly to the downside so long as the financial sector remains unsettled". The forecast marked a slowdown from 3.4% in 2022, but predicted growth could rise modestly to 3.0% in 2024. The IMF had been cutting its forecast since spring 2022.

Source: Wikipedia on USA 2023 banking crisis.

During this time, it was curious to see how markets reacted with the price of Bitcoin (BTC) increasing based on the fact that no one was secure to put their funds into the banking system if there were a systematical risk.

Not even with the FDIC that has a top of 250k per account holder.

FDIC (Federal Deposit Insurance Corporation) insured refers to the protection provided to depositors in U.S. banks and savings associations. The FDIC is a federal agency established to maintain stability and public confidence in the nation's financial system. Here's what you need to know about FDIC insurance:

Deposit Protection: FDIC insurance protects depositors against the loss of their insured deposits if an FDIC-insured bank or savings association fails. It covers deposits in checking accounts, savings accounts, certificates of deposit (CDs), and money market accounts, up to specified limits.

Coverage Limits: As of my last knowledge update in September 2021, the standard insurance coverage limit was $250,000 per depositor, per insured bank, for each account ownership category. This means that if you have more than $250,000 in one bank, you may want to consider structuring your accounts to maximize your coverage.

Types of Accounts: FDIC insurance covers a wide range of deposit accounts, including single accounts, joint accounts, revocable trust accounts, and certain retirement accounts (like IRAs).

Not All Investments: It's important to note that FDIC insurance covers only deposits. Investments such as stocks, bonds, mutual funds, and annuities are not insured by the FDIC. Additionally, the contents of safe deposit boxes are not covered.

Financial Stability: The existence of FDIC insurance contributes to the stability of the U.S. banking system by reassuring depositors that their funds are protected, reducing the likelihood of bank runs.

No Cost to Depositors: FDIC insurance does not cost depositors; it is funded by premiums paid by banks and savings associations that are insured by the FDIC.

Here is the question, why is there a limit only to guarantee or insure only up to USD 250.000? With this money you cannot even buy a new average price home in USA today in 2023.

It only means that the banking system now a day has a lot of issues and flaws depending on the economic cycles and measures provided by central banks that affects various areas of an economic functioning system.

Here is a brief example:

GLOBAL DEBT TO GDP RATIO BY COUNTRY IN 2023

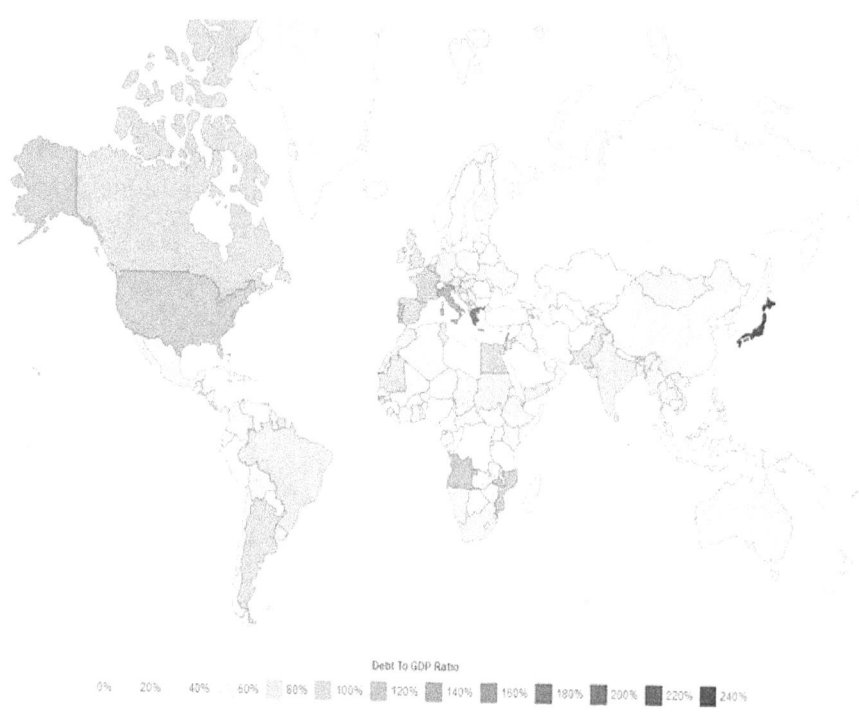

Source: World Bank Statistics

-**Japan** has one of the highest debt ratio at **around 220%** being a developed country. An aging population has strained public finances, requiring increased spending on healthcare, pensions, and social security. These mounting expenses have exacerbated the debt burden. Furthermore, Japan's economy has been plagued by a lack of productivity growth and structural issues.

-**Russia** has one of the lowest debt ratio at around 17%. With a GDP of around 2.1 trillion USD.

-**USA** being a superpower has +120% debt to GDP ratio with a GDP of 27 trillion USD.

USA DEBT TO GDP RATIO HISTORICAL

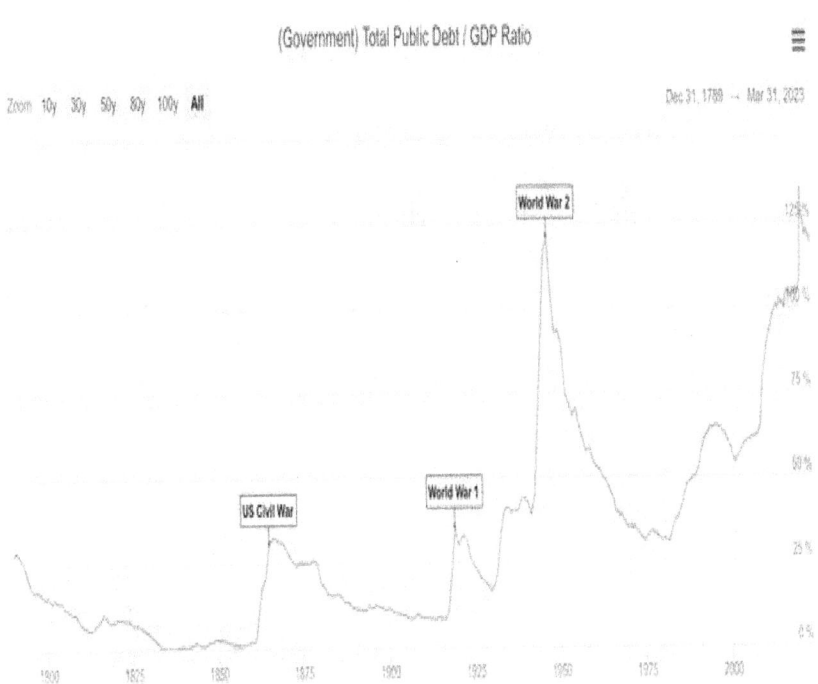

Source: World Bank Statistics

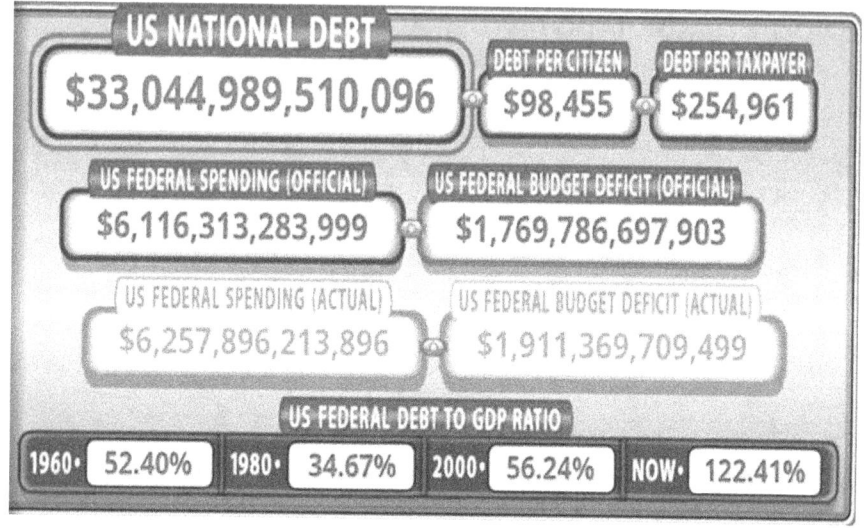

Source: https://www.usdebtclock.org/ as of late September 2023.

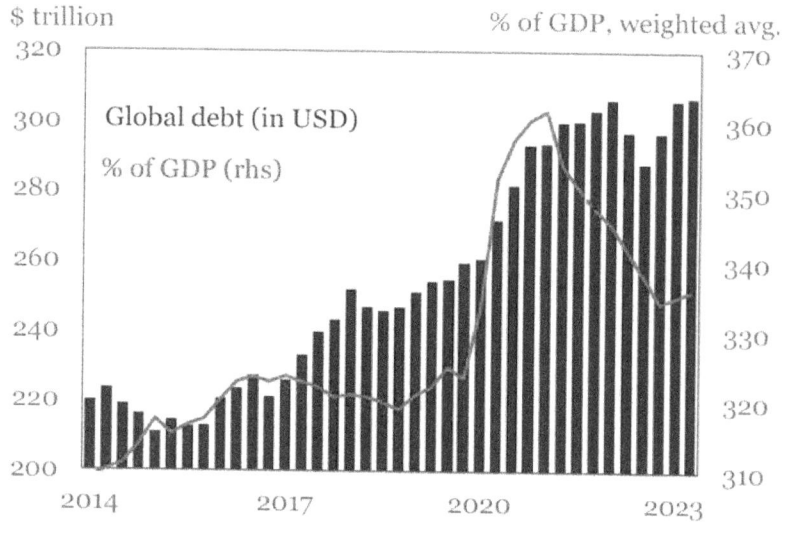

Source: World Economic Outlook Report IMF.

This means that the entire world produces or its economy size it is 105 Trillion USD and as the global debt sits at around 310 trillion USD, the global weighted average debt ratio it is +300%

Debt-to-GDP ratio it is a simple metric that compares a countries public debt to its economic output. The higher a countries debt to GDP ratio is, the higher the risk of that country to default on its debt, therefore creating a financial panic in the international markets.

This leads to think to whom do we owe this much amount of money? You could say or answer that the debt it is to ourselves. It just basically tells us that there was a much greater need of funding with in the world's economy since many years back to being able to develop countries infrastructure and all related to government plans.

This also is telling us that to rely on taxes as a revenue source it is not efficient, not enough and that there has to be a completely different approach to this matter.

For example, USA has been struggling for many years with government shut downs, just because of the debt ceiling. We come again to the same point where revenue it is not enough and there is no solution to its ever mounting debt as long as with increasing interest payments. Seems like a never ending spiral to the grave.

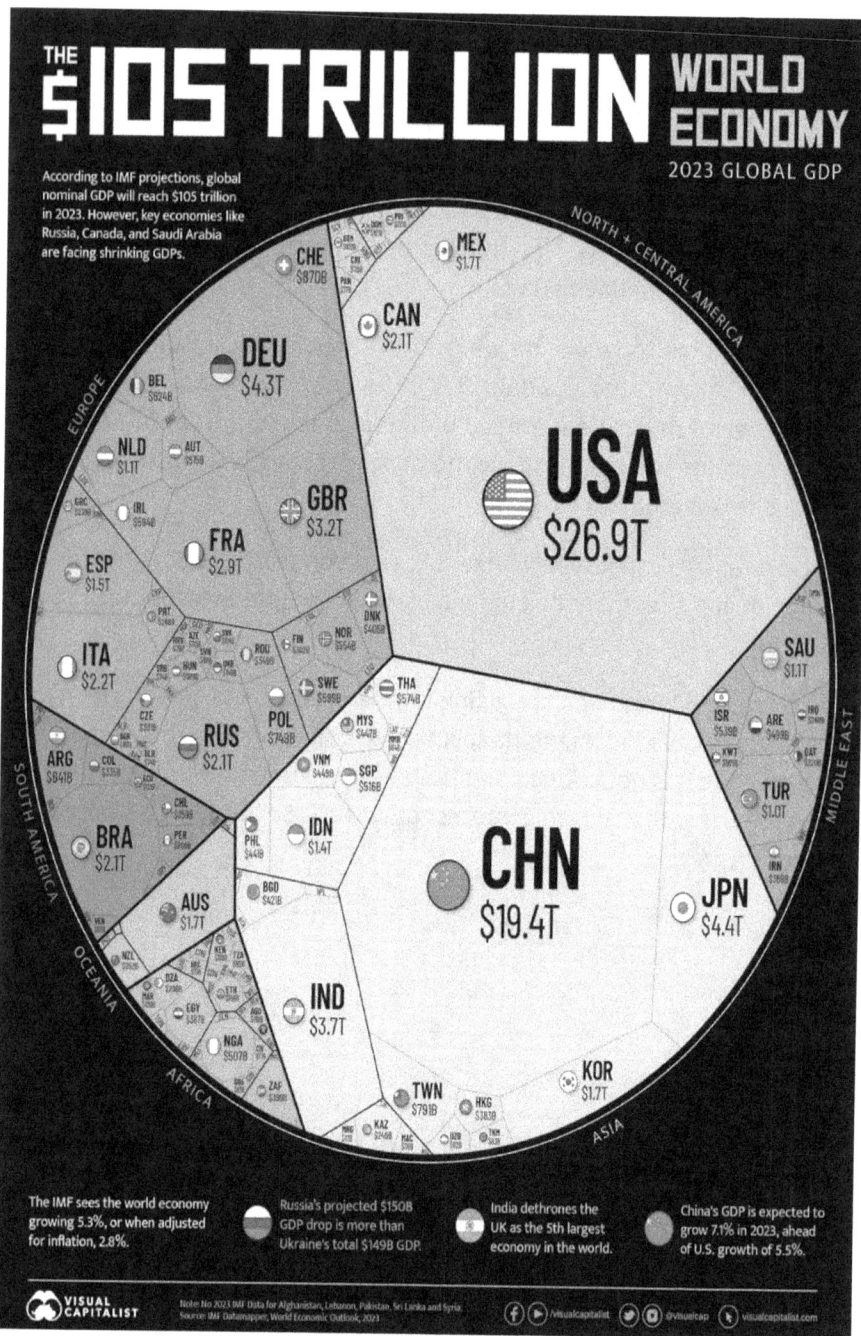

GLOBAL CURRENCIES Vs USD LAST 10 YEARS.

Currency	Ticker	10-Yr Return	Currency	Ticker	10-Yr Return	Currency	Ticker	10-Yr Return	Currency	Ticker	10-Yr Return
Venezuelan Bolivar	VEF	-99.9998%	Mongolian Tughrik	MNT	-53.4%	Malaysian Ringgit	MYR	-31.3%	Macedonian Denar	MKD	-22.0%
Sudanese Pound	SDG	-99.3%	Colombian Peso	COP	-53.2%	Mauritian Rupee	MUR	-30.5%	Guinean Franc	GNF	-21.1%
Syrian Pound	SYP	-99.1%	Malagasy Ariary	MGA	-50.5%	Romanian Leu	RON	-30.5%	South Korean Won	KRW	-20.8%
Argentine Peso	ARS	-98.3%	Tunisian Dinar	TND	-48.5%	Bangladeshi Taka	BDT	-29.4%	Moroccan Dirham	MAD	-19.9%
Turkish Lira	TRY	-92.6%	Namibian Dollar	NAD	-47.6%	Polish Zloty	PLN	-29.1%	Fijian Dollar	FJD	-18.6%
Surinamese Dollar	SRD	-91.5%	Basotho Loti	LSL	-47.6%	Afghan Afghani	AFN	-29.0%	Turkmenistani Manat	TMT	-18.4%
Angolan Kwanza	AOA	-88.2%	Swazi Lilangeni	SZL	-47.6%	Papua New Guinean Kina	PGK	-28.8%	Czech Koruna	CZK	-17.9%
North Korean Won	KPW	-85.9%	South African Rand	ZAR	-47.6%	Moldovan Leu	MDL	-28.6%	Honduran Lempira	HNL	-17.5%
Uzbekistani Som	UZS	-82.4%	Burundian Franc	BIF	-45.9%	New Zealand Dollar	NZD	-28.3%	Samoan Tala	WST	-16.2%
Ghanaian Cedi	GHS	-81.3%	Gambian Dalasi	GMD	-45.7%	Peruvian Sol	PEN	-26.9%	Chinese Yuan Renminbi	CNY	-16.2%
Sierra Leonean Leone	SLL	-81.0%	Rwandan Franc	RWF	-45.3%	Indonesian Rupiah	IDR	-26.3%	Solomon Islander Dollar	SBD	-16.1%
Nigerian Naira	NGN	-79.5%	Kyrgyzstani Som	KGS	-45.1%	Mexican Peso	MXN	-25.7%	Thai Baht	THB	-14.6%
Ukrainian Hryvnia	UAH	-77.9%	Chilean Peso	CLP	-44.6%	Nepalese Rupee	NPR	-25.6%	Yemeni Rial	YER	-14.2%
Egyptian Pound	EGP	-77.7%	Norwegian Krone	NOK	-44.2%	Dominican Peso	DOP	-25.0%	Vietnamese Dong	VND	-13.2%
Libyan Dinar	LYD	-74.5%	Uruguayan Peso	UYU	-43.9%	British Pound	GBP	-24.8%	Icelandic Krona	ISK	-12.1%
Kazakhstani Tenge	KZT	-67.9%	Swedish Krona	SEK	-41.9%	Tongan Pa'anga	TOP	-24.7%	Iraqi Dinar	IQD	-11.1%
Haitian Gourde	HTG	-67.6%	Kenyan Shilling	KES	-41.4%	Bhutanese Ngultrum	BTN	-24.7%	Singapore Dollar	SGD	-9.5%
Russian Ruble	RUB	-66.7%	Iranian Rial	IRR	-41.0%	Indian Rupee	INR	-24.7%	Bruneian Dollar	BND	-8.5%
Malawian Kwacha	MWK	-66.4%	Hungarian Forint	HUF	-41.0%	Serbian Dinar	RSD	-24.0%	Kuwaiti Dinar	KWD	-8.4%
Ethiopian Birr	ETB	-65.8%	Algerian Dinar	DZD	-40.2%	Philippine Peso	PHP	-23.9%	Israeli Shekel	ILS	-7.5%
Pakistani Rupee	PKR	-63.6%	Paraguayan Guarani	PYG	-39.0%	Canadian Dollar	CAD	-23.8%	Costa Rican Colon	CRC	-5.7%
Congolese Franc	CDF	-63.4%	Georgian Lari	GEL	-37.9%	Cape Verdean Escudo	CVE	-23.5%	Trinidadian Dollar	TTD	-5.1%
Lao Kip	LAK	-61.1%	Botswana Pula	BWP	-37.2%	Euro	EUR	-22.4%	Guyanese Dollar	GYD	-2.9%
Sri Lankan Rupee	LKR	-58.3%	Tanzanian Shilling	TZS	-35.9%	Comorian Franc	KMF	-22.4%	Belizean Dollar	BZD	-1.9%
Liberian Dollar	LRD	-57.9%	Japanese Yen	JPY	-34.3%	Central African CFA Franc	XAF	-22.4%	Swiss Franc	CHF	-1.6%
Tajikistani Somoni	TJS	-56.6%	Jamaican Dollar	JMD	-33.6%	Bosnian Convertible Mark	BAM	-22.4%	Bitcoin	BTC	21,389%
Brazilian Real	BRL	-55.4%	Nicaraguan Cordoba	NIO	-32.0%	CFP Franc	XPF	-22.4%			
Azerbaijani Manat	AZN	-53.9%	Australian Dollar	AUD	-31.7%	Bulgarian Lev	BGN	-22.4%			
Burmese Kyat	MMK	-53.6%	Tuvaluan Dollar	TVD	-31.7%	Danish Krone	DKK	-22.3%			
Mozambican Metical	MZN	-53.4%	Ugandan Shilling	UGX	-31.6%	Ni-Vanuatu Vatu	VUV	-22.1%			

Source: XE markets

Globalization has had a profound impact on taxes and currencies, reshaping the way countries collect revenue and manage their monetary systems. Here are some key ways in which globalization has influenced these aspects:

Taxes:

Tax Evasion and Avoidance: Globalization has made it easier for individuals and multinational corporations to engage in tax evasion and avoidance. The mobility of capital and income across borders allows entities to exploit tax havens, shifting profits to low-tax jurisdictions and reducing their overall tax liability.

Transfer Pricing: Multinational corporations often engage in transfer pricing, manipulating the prices of goods and services transferred between their subsidiaries in different countries to minimize tax liabilities. This practice has led to challenges in enforcing fair taxation.

Tax Competition: To attract foreign investment and remain competitive in the global economy, many countries have lowered their corporate tax rates. This tax competition can lead to a race to the bottom, reducing the overall revenue that governments collect from corporate taxes.

Global Taxation Reform: In response to the challenges posed by globalization, international efforts have emerged to reform the global tax system. Initiatives like the Base Erosion and Profit Shifting (BEPS) project by the OECD aim to address issues related to tax avoidance and ensure that profits are taxed where economic activities take place.

Digital Economy Taxation: The rise of digital commerce and remote work has posed challenges for taxation. Countries are exploring ways to tax digital services and remote work income, often leading to debates about how to fairly allocate tax revenues across borders.

Currencies:

Exchange Rates and Currency Markets: Globalization has increased the importance of exchange rates and currency markets. Fluctuations in exchange rates can impact international trade, investment, and capital flows. Central banks and governments often intervene to manage their currency's value and stability.

Dollarization: In some countries, the U.S. dollar has become the de facto currency due to its stability and wide acceptance in global trade. This practice, known as dollarization, reduces a country's control over its monetary policy.

Global Reserve Currencies: The U.S. dollar and the euro are dominant global reserve currencies. They are held by central banks and international institutions as a means of conducting international transactions and storing value.

Currency Pegs and Fixed Exchange Rates: Some countries choose to peg their currencies to another currency (usually the U.S. dollar or euro) to maintain stability and boost investor confidence. These fixed exchange rate regimes can help attract foreign investment.

Cryptocurrencies: The rise of cryptocurrencies like Bitcoin has introduced a new dimension to global currencies. While not yet a major part of the global financial system, cryptocurrencies have the potential to impact cross-border transactions and financial stability.

Currency Wars: Competitive devaluations and currency manipulation have sometimes been used by countries to gain a trade advantage. This can lead to tensions and disputes in the international economic arena.

Globalization has interconnected economies and financial systems in ways that require international cooperation and coordination in taxation and currency management. Addressing the challenges posed by globalization in these areas often requires multilateral agreements, transparency, and efforts to ensure fair and equitable outcomes for all nations.

LIMITATIONS OF GDP AS A MEASURE OF WELL-BEING

Gross Domestic Product (GDP) is a widely used economic indicator that measures the monetary value of all goods and services produced within a country's borders within a specific time period. While GDP is valuable for assessing the size and growth of an economy, it has several limitations as a measure of well-being and overall societal progress:

Excludes Non-Market Activities: GDP primarily focuses on market transactions, excluding non-market activities such as unpaid housework, caregiving, and volunteer work. These activities contribute significantly to well-being but are not captured in GDP.

Ignores Income Distribution: GDP doesn't provide information about how income and wealth are distributed within a society. A high GDP per capita may mask significant income inequality, which can lead to disparities in well-being.

Quality of Life: GDP doesn't account for the quality of life or the well-being of citizens. It doesn't consider factors like healthcare access, education quality, safety, or environmental conditions, which are essential for overall well-being.

Environmental Costs: GDP doesn't deduct the negative environmental costs associated with economic growth. It can lead to the unsustainable use of natural resources and environmental degradation, which can harm long-term well-being.

Ignores Household Debt: Rising household debt can contribute to increased consumer spending, which may boost GDP in the short term. However, it doesn't account for the potential negative consequences of high levels of household debt on well-being.

Innovation and Technology: GDP doesn't capture the full benefits of innovation and technological advancement. While these advancements can enhance well-being, GDP only measures their impact in terms of increased economic output.

Quality vs. Quantity: GDP doesn't distinguish between goods and services of varying quality. It treats all output equally, which can lead to an overemphasis on quantity over quality.

Informal Economy: Many countries have substantial informal or underground economies that go unaccounted for in GDP calculations. These unreported economic activities can significantly affect well-being but aren't reflected in GDP.

Externalities: GDP doesn't account for externalities, such as pollution or the depletion of natural resources, which can have negative impacts on well-being. These costs are often borne by society and future generations.

Subjective Well-being: GDP doesn't measure subjective well-being or happiness, which is an essential component of overall societal welfare. People's perceptions of their well-being may not align with economic growth.

Cultural and Social Factors: GDP doesn't consider cultural and social factors that influence well-being. Cultural values, social cohesion, and community well-being are not accounted for in GDP.

Long-Term Sustainability: GDP doesn't provide information on the long-term sustainability of economic growth. It can't assess whether current growth patterns can be maintained without jeopardizing future generations' well-being.

Given these limitations, policymakers and researchers often complement GDP with other indicators and metrics, such as the Human Development Index (HDI), Genuine Progress Indicator (GPI), and various well-being indices. These alternative measures provide a more comprehensive view of societal well-being by considering factors beyond economic output and income.

GOVERNMENT ASSETS: AN UNDERUTILIZED RESOURCE

Government assets, which include public infrastructure, land, natural resources, and other holdings, are valuable resources that can play a significant role in a country's economic development and fiscal sustainability. However, they are often underutilized or not managed optimally. Here are some reasons why government assets are considered an underutilized resource and their potential benefits when managed effectively:

1. Poor Asset Management:

Many governments struggle with inefficient asset management practices, leading to underutilization and waste of valuable resources. Assets may not be adequately maintained, upgraded, or utilized to their full potential.

2. Lack of Transparency:

In some cases, government assets may not be well-documented or reported transparently. This can hinder effective decision-making and lead to misallocation or underutilization of resources.

3. Fiscal Challenges:

In times of fiscal challenges, governments may prioritize short-term revenue generation over long-term asset management. This can result in the sale of valuable assets to address immediate budgetary concerns.

4. Infrastructure Gaps:

Many countries face significant infrastructure gaps, such as inadequate transportation systems, water and sanitation facilities, and energy infrastructure. Properly managing and leveraging existing assets can help address these gaps more cost-effectively.

5. Economic Development:

Government assets, such as land and industrial zones, can be used strategically to attract investments and stimulate economic development. Well-planned industrial parks, for example, can create jobs and generate revenue.

6. Environmental Stewardship:

Natural resources owned by governments, including forests and minerals, need to be managed sustainably to protect the environment and ensure long-term benefits.

7. Revenue Generation:

Governments can generate revenue from government-owned enterprises, public-private partnerships (PPPs), and leasing or selling underutilized assets. These funds can be reinvested in public services and infrastructure.

8. Public Service Delivery:

Government assets like buildings and facilities can be repurposed to improve public service delivery. For instance, vacant government buildings can be used as community centers, schools, or healthcare facilities.

9. Social Housing and Affordable Housing Initiatives:

Government-owned land can be used to address housing challenges, including the development of social and affordable housing projects.

10. Cultural and Heritage Preservation:

- Historical and cultural assets can be preserved and promoted for tourism and cultural enrichment, contributing to both economic and societal well-being.

11. Infrastructure Resilience:

- Investing in infrastructure resilience, such as upgrading and maintaining roads and bridges, can mitigate the impact of natural disasters and climate change.

12. Long-Term Sustainability:

- Proper management of government assets ensures their sustainability for future generations, preserving the value of these resources over time.

To harness the potential of government assets fully, governments must prioritize transparent asset management, develop long-term asset management strategies, and consider the broader economic, social, and environmental impacts of their decisions. This requires a comprehensive approach that balances immediate financial needs with long-term sustainability and societal well-being.

DOLLARIZATION OF THE ECONOMY

Dollarization, or the adoption of a foreign currency, typically the United States dollar, as the official or de facto currency of an economy, can have several significant economic and financial impacts on a country. Here are some of the key factors to take into account:

1. Exchange Rate Stability:

One of the primary motivations for dollarization is to achieve exchange rate stability. By using a stable foreign currency like the U.S. dollar, a country can reduce the risk of currency devaluation and exchange rate fluctuations, which can be particularly beneficial for international trade and attracting foreign investment.

2. Inflation Control:

Dollarization can help control inflation, as the country relinquishes its ability to print its own money. This can be especially valuable if the domestic currency has a history of high inflation. A stable currency can promote price stability and economic predictability.

3. Lower Interest Rates:

A stable foreign currency can lead to lower interest rates because it reduces the risk premium typically associated with lending and borrowing in an unstable domestic currency. This can stimulate investment and economic growth.

4. Attraction of Foreign Investment:

Dollarization can make a country more attractive to foreign investors, as they are more likely to invest in an economy with a stable and widely accepted currency.

5. Easier Trade and Investment:

Adopting the U.S. dollar can facilitate trade and investment with countries that use the same currency, as it eliminates the need for foreign exchange transactions and uncertainties in exchange rates fluctuations.

6. Enhanced Financial Credibility:

Dollarization can enhance a country's financial credibility and creditworthiness, making it easier to access international financial markets.

7. Reduced Transaction Costs:

The elimination of exchange rate risk can reduce transaction costs for businesses engaged in international trade.

8. Economic Policy Constraints:

Dollarization limits a country's ability to pursue independent monetary and exchange rate policies. It relies on the policies of the currency-issuing country (in this case, the United States).

9. Fiscal Constraints:

Governments may need to be more fiscally disciplined when using a foreign currency, as they can't rely on monetary policy (printing money) to finance budget deficits. This can lead to reduced fiscal flexibility.

10. Income Distribution:

- Dollarization can impact income distribution, as it may lead to a concentration of wealth and benefits in sectors or individuals closely tied to international trade and investment.

11. Challenges in Financial Crises:

- In a financial crisis, dollarized countries may not have the same tools available to deal with the crisis as countries with their own currency. They are dependent on the policies of the currency-issuing country.

It's important to note that dollarization is not a one-size-fits-all solution. Its impact depends on the specific circumstances and the policies implemented by the adopting country. While it offers potential benefits, it also comes with constraints and trade-offs, particularly in terms of monetary and fiscal policy independence. Countries considering dollarization must carefully weigh the pros and cons based on their economic and financial conditions.

It could be also a little bit contradictory, once the USA it is the most taxed country and taxed economy in the world.

IMPLICATIONS ON THE GLOBAL ECONOMY FROM AI AND ROBOTICS.

The implications of AI (Artificial Intelligence) and robotics for the global economy over the next 10-20 years are wide-ranging and significant. Let's take a look at some potential impacts to consider:

1. Automation of Jobs:

AI and robotics will likely lead to increased automation of various jobs across different sectors, including manufacturing, transportation, retail, healthcare, and finance. While this can improve efficiency and productivity, it may also result in job displacement and require workers to adapt to new roles or acquire new skills.

In this case, what or whom will the government tax? The machines or the corporations and what will happen to the people displaced by these robots?

2. Economic Growth and Productivity:

AI and robotics have the potential to boost economic growth and productivity by streamlining processes, reducing costs, and enabling innovations in various industries. Businesses that adopt these technologies effectively may gain a competitive advantage in the global market.

3. New Job Opportunities:

While automation may eliminate certain jobs, it can also create new job opportunities in emerging fields related to AI, robotics, data science, and cybersecurity. There will be a growing demand for skilled professionals who can develop, implement, and maintain AI and robotic systems.

4. Skills and Education:

The rise of AI and robotics will require a workforce with advanced technical skills, critical thinking abilities, and adaptability. Education systems will need to evolve to provide individuals with the necessary training and education to succeed in a digital and automated economy.

5. Income Inequality:

The adoption of AI and robotics may exacerbate income inequality if certain segments of the population, particularly low-skilled workers, are disproportionately affected by job displacement. Addressing these disparities may require policy interventions, such as upskilling programs and social safety nets.

6. Disruption of Industries:

AI and robotics have the potential to disrupt entire industries, leading to the restructuring of value chains, changes in business models, and the emergence of new market leaders. Established companies may need to adapt quickly to remain competitive in a rapidly evolving landscape.

7. Ethical and Regulatory Challenges:

The widespread adoption of AI and robotics raises ethical considerations regarding privacy, security, bias, and accountability. Governments and regulatory bodies will need to develop appropriate frameworks to address these challenges and ensure that these technologies are deployed responsibly.

8. Global Competition and Geopolitics:

Countries that invest heavily in AI research and development may gain a competitive edge in the global economy. The race for AI supremacy could lead to geopolitical tensions and shape international relations in the coming years.

9. Economic Disruptions and Transition Periods:

The transition to a more automated economy may involve short-term economic disruptions, job losses, and adjustments in labor markets. Governments, businesses, and communities will need to manage this transition effectively to minimize negative impacts and maximize opportunities.

10. Environmental Impact:

- AI and robotics have the potential to improve resource efficiency and sustainability in various industries, leading to positive environmental outcomes. However, they may also contribute to energy consumption and carbon emissions, particularly if not deployed responsibly.

Overall, the widespread adoption of AI and robotics will have profound implications for the global economy, reshaping industries, labor markets, and societal structures. While these technologies offer immense potential for innovation and growth, they also pose challenges that will require careful consideration and proactive responses from policymakers, businesses, and society as a whole.

KENYA REPLACES NUMERICAL DEBT CEILING WITH LIMIT AT 55% OF GDP

Kenya has approved changes to the way it determines the maximum amount of debt the government can hold, as it seeks to improve transparency in the accounting and management of the country's loans.

Kenya borrowed the largest amount of money in a single year during President William Ruto's first year in office, pushing the debt levels past the ceiling amid shortfalls in tax collections and increased repayment obligations.

Gross debt stock climbed Ksh1.56 trillion ($10.8 billion) for the financial year ended June, fresh data released by the Treasury shows, breaching the Ksh10 trillion ($69.52 billion) mark by Ksh189.53 billion ($1.32 billion).

Kenya ended the last financial year in June with a gross total debt load of Ksh10.19 trillion ($70.84 billion), a growth of 18.08 percent over Ksh8.63 trillion ($59.99 billion) a year ago, which was the last full fiscal year for former president Uhuru Kenyatta.

Read: Kenya debt costs fall $1.63bn on cheaper loansLawmakers in June voted to convert the numerical debt ceiling to an anchor of 55 percent of gross domestic product (GDP), with the Treasury given five years to comply.

The jump in gross debt came in a fiscal year Dr Ruto, who was in charge for nine of the 12 months under review, made it clear his administration would cut borrowing.

Nearly Ksh1.43 trillion ($9.94 billion), or 91.52 percent, of the new gross debt, was contracted in the last nine months of the year under review, according to the Treasury data.

Dr Ruto, who partly rode to power on a pledge to make debt a "last resort" in raising funds to plug holes in the budget, had pledged not to make the nation "slaves of debt from any place or any country".

He vowed to pursue policies, which enhance tax compliance levels and grow national savings from a measly "seven" percent of GDP towards 30 percent envisioned in Kenya's long-term development blueprint, Vision 2030."I am looking forward to the day, soon enough, when we borrow from the savings of the people of Kenya to run our development instead of borrowing from other countries, and that is what holds the future for us," Dr Ruto had said last September ahead of being sworn into office."I am encouraging the people of Kenya as we work together to get our economy out of the mud... that each and every one of us must pay their taxes and I am going to lead from the front, making sure I pay my taxes. "Provisional official data, however, suggests the Ruto administration's fiscal consolidation plan was roiled by underperformance in the main tax streams, which missed the Ksh2 trillion ($13.9 billion) by Ksh112.76 billion ($783.9 million) in an environment of a softening economy.

Foreign borrowing accounted for two-thirds of the jump in gross debt after Kenya contracted an additional Ksh1.06 trillion ($7.37 billion) from foreign creditors to stand at Ksh5.36 trillion ($37.26 billion).

Multilateral lenders — largely the World Bank Group, the International Monetary Fund (IMF) and African Development Bank (AfDB) — grew their credit to Kenya by Ksh728.85 billion ($5.1 billion), or 37.89 percent year-on-year, zooming past the Ksh2.65 trillion ($18.42 billion) mark.

Read: IMF, World Bank fingerprints on Kenya's $26bn BudgetLoans from multilateral lenders such as the World Bank and AfDB come on concessional terms, which average a 1.75 percent fixed interest rate, with a 35-year tenor and a grace period of up to 10 years.

This eases the burden of future repayments, unlike commercial borrowing like Eurobond where the interest rates are higher, currently double-digit, with shorter tenors.

The stock of debt taken from foreign commercial banks and rich countries increased by Ksh166.09 billion ($1.15 billion) and Ksh159.83 billion ($1.11 billion) in the review period, partly reflecting the impact of a weaker shilling, to close at Ksh1.36 trillion ($9.45 billion) and Ksh1.33 trillion ($9.25 billion).

Borrowings sourced from domestic sources such as commercial banks, pension funds and insurers through the sale of Treasury bonds and bills increased Ksh503.01 billion ($3.5 billion) to end June 2023 at Ksh4.83 trillion ($33.58 billion).

The IMF and the World Bank have since 2020 classified Kenya at a high risk of debt distress since 2020 as a result of persistently large deficits in annual budgets in more than a decade, which are bridged through borrowing.

Read: Ruto appeals to World Bank, IMF for Africa debt reliefKenya's debt binge is underlined by Eurobond offerings, a package of Chinese loans and syndicated commercial loans over the years which are now squeezing its finances as the loans fall due.

The Ruto administration, for example, spent Ksh1.16 trillion ($8.06 billion) on servicing maturing debt and interest for the year ended June, with the burden projected to rise to an estimated Ksh1.8 trillion ($12.51 billion) in the current year ending June 2024."I do believe that the fiscal framework of the National Treasury has incorporated all these debt service payments, including the impact of a higher exchange rate," CBK Governor Kamau Thugge said on June 26."They have a plan to reduce the overall fiscal deficit and to achieve a sustainable debt position and fiscal position over the medium term."

Source: https://www.zawya.com/en/economy/africa/kenyas-debt-up-record-108bln-m2ezmimq

ARGENTINA'S ECONOMIC TROUBLES.

Argentina has experienced chronic inflation and currency devaluation over the past several decades due to a combination of economic, fiscal, and monetary factors. Here are some of the key reasons behind Argentina's persistent inflation and devaluation:

1. Fiscal Mismanagement:

- One of the primary causes of Argentina's economic challenges is fiscal mismanagement, including high government deficits and debt levels. Overspending and budget deficits have forced the government to print money to cover its expenses, leading to inflation.

2. Monetary Policy Issues:

- Argentina has often pursued loose monetary policies, including excessive money supply growth. A growing money supply can lead to inflation, eroding the value of the currency.

3. Exchange Rate Policies:

- Frequent changes in exchange rate policies have contributed to instability. Argentina has alternated between fixed exchange rate regimes, currency pegs, and periods of floating exchange rates. These shifts have often resulted in abrupt devaluations when policies are unsustainable.

4. External Debt:

- Argentina's history of accumulating external debt, including sovereign debt defaults, has created uncertainty in global financial markets. Debt repayments and negotiations have at times strained the country's fiscal position and contributed to devaluation.

5. Political Instability:

- Frequent political changes and shifts in government policies have added to economic uncertainty. Political decisions have often prioritized short-term goals over long-term economic stability.

•

6. Lack of Confidence:

- A lack of confidence in the stability of the Argentine economy has led to capital flight, which further weakens the currency and fuels inflation.

7. Commodity Price Fluctuations:

- Argentina's economy is heavily reliant on the export of agricultural commodities, which are subject to price fluctuations in global markets. Variations in commodity prices can affect the country's trade balance and currency stability.

8. Inefficient Subsidies:

- Subsidies on energy, utilities, and transportation have been a significant fiscal burden on the government. These subsidies, while aimed at protecting consumers, have contributed to fiscal deficits and inflation.

9. Wage-Price Spirals:

- High inflation has often triggered wage-price spirals, where workers demand higher wages to keep pace with rising prices, leading to further inflationary pressures.

10. Inadequate Structural Reforms: - Argentina has struggled to implement necessary structural reforms in areas like taxation, labor markets, and public spending. These reforms are crucial for long-term economic stability.

11. Dollarization and Black Market: - Due to inflation and currency devaluation, many Argentines have turned to the U.S. dollar as a more stable store of value. This has led to a thriving informal market for foreign exchange.

Addressing Argentina's inflation and devaluation challenges requires a comprehensive approach that includes fiscal discipline, monetary stability, structural reforms, and consistent economic policies. Achieving long-term stability and restoring confidence in the Argentine economy remains a complex and ongoing process.

A NOTE ON USA DEBT AND INTEREST PAYMENTS FOR THE YEARS TO COME.

Interest payments on the $33.7 trillion in US national debt is now annualized at over $1.0 trillion per year. This is the 2nd largest item in the budget, behind only social security. Interest on the debt is now more than Defense. With $6 trillion in debt maturing in the next 12 months, much of that old debt at 1% to 2% rates will have to rollover and be refinanced at the current rates of 5%. 12 months from now, if rates are 5% or higher, we will likely be paying $1.3 trillion per year in interest on the debt. If the debt grows to $40 trillion within 2 years and it all gets refinanced at 5% or higher, interest payments on the debt could be $2 trillion per year by 2026.

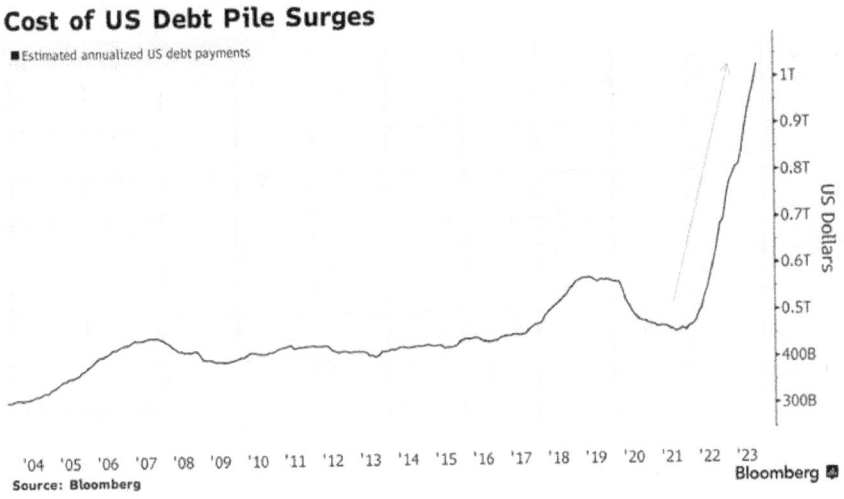

Keep in mind ... all personal income taxes collected in the USA is only about $2.5 trillion per year. Total government revenue from all sources is around $5 trillion per year.

Source: @WallStreetSilv on X - 8th of November 2023.

INTERNATIONAL TAX COMPETITIVENESS INDEX 2023

The structure of a country's tax code is a determining factor of its economic performance. A well-structured tax code is easy for taxpayers to comply with and can promote economic development while raising sufficient revenue for a government's priorities. In contrast, poorly structured tax systems can be costly, distort economic decision-making, and harm domestic economies. Many countries have recognized this and have reformed their tax codes. Over the past few decades, marginal tax rates on corporate and individual income have declined significantly across the Organization for Economic Co-operation and Development (OECD). Now, most OECD nations raise a significant amount of revenue from broad-based taxes such as payroll taxes and value-added taxes (VAT).1 Not all recent changes in tax policy among OECD countries have improved the structure of tax systems; some have made a negative impact. Though some countries like the United States and France have reduced their corporate income tax rates by several percentage points, others, like Colombia, have increased them. Corporate tax base improvements have occurred in Portugal, while the corporate tax base has been made less competitive in Belgium. The United States, the United Kingdom, and Chile are phasing out temporary improvements to their corporate tax bases. The COVID-19 pandemic has led many countries to adopt temporary changes to their tax systems. Faced with revenue shortfalls from the downturn, countries will need to consider how to best structure their tax systems to foster both an economic recovery and raise revenue. The variety of approaches to taxation among OECD countries creates a need to evaluate these systems relative to each other. For that purpose, we have developed the International Tax Competitiveness Index—a relative comparison of OECD countries' tax systems with respect to competitiveness and neutrality.

The International Tax Competitiveness Index (ITCI) seeks to measure the extent to which a country's tax system adheres to two important aspects of tax policy: competitiveness and neutrality. A competitive tax code is one that keeps marginal tax rates low. In today's globalized world, capital is highly mobile. Businesses can choose to invest in any number of countries throughout the world to find the highest rate of return. This means that businesses will look for countries with lower tax rates on investment to maximize their after-tax rate of return. If a country's tax rate is too high, it will drive investment elsewhere, leading to slower economic growth. In addition, high marginal tax rates can impede domestic investment and lead to tax avoidance. According to research from the OECD, corporate taxes are most harmful for economic growth, with personal income taxes and consumption taxes being less harmful. Taxes on immovable property have the smallest impact on growth.

Separately, a neutral tax code is simply one that seeks to raise the most revenue with the fewest economic distortions. This means that it doesn't favor consumption over saving, as happens with investment taxes and wealth taxes. It also means few or no targeted tax breaks for specific activities carried out by businesses or individuals. As tax laws become more complex, they also become less neutral. If, in theory, the same taxes apply to all businesses and individuals, but the rules are such that large businesses or wealthy individuals can change their behavior to gain a tax advantage, this undermines the neutrality of a tax system. A tax code that is competitive and neutral promotes sustainable economic growth and investment while raising sufficient revenue for government priorities. There are many factors unrelated to taxes which affect a country's economic performance. Nevertheless, taxes play an important role in the health of a country's economy. To measure whether a country's tax system is neutral and competitive, the ITCI looks at more than 40 tax policy variables. These variables measure not only the level of tax rates, but also how taxes are structured. The Index looks at a country's corporate taxes, individual income taxes, consumption taxes, property taxes, and the treatment of profits earned overseas. The ITCI gives a comprehensive overview of how developed countries' tax codes compare, explains why certain tax codes stand out as good or bad models for reform, and provides important insight into how to think about tax policy. Due to some data limitations, recent tax changes in some countries may not be reflected in this year's version of the International Tax Competitiveness Index.

2023 Rankings

For the 10th year in a row, Estonia has the best tax code in the OECD. Its top score is driven by four positive features of its tax system. First, it has a 20 percent tax rate on corporate income that is only applied to distributed profits. Second, it has a flat 20 percent tax on individual income that does not apply to personal dividend income. Third, its property tax applies only to the value of land, rather than to the value of real property or capital. Finally, it has a territorial tax system that exempts 100 percent of foreign profits earned by domestic corporations from domestic taxation, with few restrictions. While Estonia's tax system is the most competitive in the OECD, the other top countries' tax systems receive high scores due to excellence in one or more of the major tax categories. Latvia, which recently adopted the Estonian system for corporate taxation, also has a relatively efficient system for taxing labor income. New Zealand has a relatively flat, low-rate individual income tax that also largely exempts capital gains (with a combined top rate of 39 percent), a broad-based VAT , and levies no taxes on inheritance, property transfers, assets, or financial transactions. Switzerland has a relatively low corporate tax rate (19.7 percent), a low, broad-based consumption tax, and an individual income tax that partially exempts capital gains from taxation. Luxembourg has a broad-based consumption tax and a competitive international tax system.

Colombia has the least competitive tax system in the OECD. It has a net wealth tax, a financial transaction tax, and the highest corporate income tax rate of 35 percent. Colombia's VAT covers less than 40 percent of final consumption, revealing both policy and enforcement gaps.

Italy has the second-least competitive tax system in the OECD. It has multiple distortionary property taxes with separate levies on real estate transfers, estates, and financial transactions, as well as a wealth tax on selected assets. Italy's relatively high VAT rate of 22 percent applies to the fifth-narrowest consumption tax base in the OECD. Countries that rank poorly on the ITCI often levy relatively high marginal tax rates on corporate income or have multiple layers of tax rules that contribute to complexity. The five countries at the bottom of the rankings all have higher than average combined corporate tax rates. Ireland ranks poorly on the ITCI despite its low corporate tax rate. This is due to high personal income and dividend taxes and a relatively narrow VAT base. The five lowest-ranking countries have unusually high corporate income tax rates, between 25.825 and 35 percent. Four out of the five lowest-ranking countries have unusually high top income tax thresholds, at 13 to 21 times the average income.

Table 1. 2023 International Tax Competitiveness Index Rankings

Country	Overall Rank	Overall Score	Corporate Tax Rank	Individual Taxes Rank	Consumption Taxes Rank	Property Taxes Rank	Cross-Border Tax Rules Rank
Estonia	1	100.0	2	1	15	1	11
Latvia	2	88.5	1	3	27	5	9
New Zealand	3	86.1	29	5	1	8	19
Switzerland	4	84.7	10	9	3	36	1
Czech Republic	5	81.2	6	4	25	6	10
Luxembourg	6	78.9	23	21	7	14	5
Turkey	7	78.6	11	7	13	22	7
Israel	8	78.3	13	23	11	11	8
Lithuania	9	76.6	3	10	30	7	22
Australia	10	75.9	32	14	9	4	21
Hungary	11	75.8	4	6	38	23	3
Slovak Republic	12	74.3	18	2	29	3	30
Sweden	13	73.3	8	20	21	10	13
Netherlands	14	70.6	25	19	16	21	4
Canada	15	69.8	24	24	8	25	15
Slovenia	16	66.6	7	13	31	24	18
Norway	17	66.6	14	27	23	15	12
Germany	18	66.6	31	35	14	12	6
Finland	19	66.5	9	25	24	19	20
Austria	20	65.3	20	30	17	16	16
United States	21	65.0	22	22	4	29	35
Costa Rica	22	64.8	36	33	5	9	31
Korea	23	61.6	26	37	2	32	26
Japan	24	61.5	30	34	6	26	25
Greece	25	61.4	19	8	33	28	23
Mexico	26	60.1	27	28	12	2	38
Belgium	27	60.0	15	11	22	30	33
Ireland	28	58.9	5	31	34	17	34
Denmark	29	58.5	17	36	20	18	29
United Kingdom	30	56.1	28	26	35	35	2
Spain	31	55.8	33	17	19	37	17
Iceland	32	55.5	12	18	28	34	32
Poland	33	55.3	16	12	36	31	27
Portugal	34	52.1	37	29	26	20	28
Chile	35	50.5	35	38	10	13	37
France	36	49.1	34	32	32	33	14
Italy	37	48.4	21	16	37	38	24
Colombia	38	46.4	38	15	18	27	36

Source:

https://taxfoundation.org/wp-content/uploads/2023/10/TF-ITCI23-Book_16-10_FV.pdf

CHAPTER IV

SOME OTHER STORIES TO THINK ABOUT

ARGENTINAS NEW ELECTED PRESIDENT.

Javier Gerardo Milei (born 22 October 1970) is an Argentine politician, economist, and author who is the president-elect of Argentina. Before entering politics, Milei gained notability as an economist, as the author of multiple books on economics and politics, and for his distinct political philosophy as a vocal proponent of the Austrian School. He critiqued the fiscal policies of various Argentine administrations and advocates reduced government spending.

As a university professor, Milei taught courses in macroeconomics, economic growth, microeconomics, and mathematics for economists. He also wrote numerous books and hosted radio programs. In 2021, Milei was elected a member of the Argentine Chamber of Deputies, representing the City of Buenos Aires for La Libertad Avanza. As a national deputy, he limited his legislative activities to voting, focusing instead on critiquing what he calls Argentina's political elite and its propensity for high government spending. Milei pledged not to raise taxes and donated his national deputy salary through a monthly raffle. He defeated economy minister Sergio Massa in the second round of the 2023 Argentine presidential election on a platform that held the ideological dominance of Peronism responsible for the ongoing Argentine economic crisis.

Milei is known for his flamboyant personality, distinctive personal style, and strong media presence. He has been described politically as a right-wing libertarian, right-wing populist, and supporter of laissez-faire capitalism, aligning specifically with minarchist and anarcho-capitalist principles. His views distinguish him in the Argentine political landscape and have garnered significant public attention and polarizing reactions. He has proposed a comprehensive overhaul of the country's fiscal and structural policies. Milei supports freedom of choice on drug policy, guns, prostitution, same-sex marriage, sexual preference, and gender identity, while opposing abortion and euthanasia. In foreign policy, he advocates for closer relations with the United States, supporting Ukraine in response to Russia's invasion, and distancing Argentina from geopolitical entanglement with China.

Javier Gerardo Milei is an economist, writer, and politician. He gained prominence for his libertarian views and outspoken critiques of government intervention in the economy. Milei has been associated with classical liberal economic policies and has criticized what he perceives as excessive government intervention, high taxes, and inflation in Argentina.

For over twenty years, Milei has been a professor of macroeconomics, economics of growth, microeconomics, and mathematics for economists. He is a specialist in economic growth and has taught several economic subjects in Argentine universities and abroad. He has written more than 50 academic papers.

Milei became the chief economist at Máxima AFJP, a private pension company; a head economist at Estudio Broda, a financial advising company; and a government consultant at the International Centre for Settlement of Investment Disputes. He was also a senior economist at HSBC Argentina. He served as chief economist at several national and international government public bodies. Since 2012, Milei has led the division of Economic Studies at Fundación Acordar, a national think tank. He is also a member of the B20 and a member of the Economic Policy Group of International Chamber of Commerce, an advisor to the G20. For 15 years, he worked at the private company Corporación América as the chief economist and financial adviser to Eduardo Eurnekian.

Milei is the author of several books, including El camino del libertario. He has a notable presence on television, with a 2018 ranking by Ejes showing him as the most interviewed economist on television, at 235 interviews and 193,347 seconds. Milei also hosted his own radio show, Demoliendo mitos (Demolishing Myths), featuring regular appearances by Alberdian economist and businessman Gustavo Lazzari and personalities like Alberdian lawyer Pablo Torres Barthe and right-libertarian political scientist María Zaldívar.

General elections

The Argentine peso plunged and interest rates were raised in the aftermath of his primary election victory, while the official dollar exchange rate rose by 20%, and the Central Bank of Argentina raised interest rates. As a result of his strong performance in the primaries, Milei was considered the front-runner in the general election. Analysts said this could lead to higher inflationary and foreign exchange pressures. According to the Eurasia Group analyst and Latin American researcher Luciano Sigalov, if Milei won the presidency, he would face governability issues due to lacking a parliamentary majority to pass the radical pro-market reforms he advocates, as well as street protests from Peronist and social movements; Sigalov said, "The likely prospect of a Milei victory and the risks from his radical policy program will generate more pressures on inflation and exchange rates. The worsening economic conditions will benefit Milei as he blames [rival] politicians for the spiraling crisis."

Milei's rise has been described within the context of the last two presidencies. Analysts described a win for Milei as a more dramatic version of the pro-business government of former president Mauricio Macri, who tried to introduce market reforms after taking office in 2015, only to clash with the political opposition and plunge headlong into a financial crisis that ended with the country asking the International Monetary Fund (IMF) for another rescue package. Fernández, Macri's successor, struggled to fix the economy amid the COVID-19 pandemic in Argentina and a severe shortage of foreign currency, leaving the country vulnerable to another debt default. Fernández is also an unpopular president and chose not to run for reelection. In August 2023, Milei said he would not end social programs, which support millions of people in a country where almost 40% of the population is impoverished; he called them "victims, not victimizers", adding that ending this type of social assistance would take up to 15 years.

On 22 October, Milei advanced to the runoff, in which he faced Massa. Milei defeated Massa in the runoff on 19 November, in what was described as a historic election in Argentina. In his victory speech, Milei pledged for a new political era. He vowed to begin "the reconstruction of Argentina" and end the country's economic decline. His prospective foreign minister Diana Mondino also announced Argentina would pause their accession to BRICS. Milei is to take office as president on 10 December.

Argentine politics

Milei argues that "the only time that pure liberalism was applied was in 1860 and we were a prosperous country." He criticized the governments of Hipólito Yrigoyen, Juan Perón, Raúl Alfonsín, Cristina Fernández de Kirchner,[130] and Alberto Fernández. Milei characterized 1930s Argentina as a fascist regime that led to Peronism and Perón's "three-legged fascism" rather than a return to liberal policies. Milei excluded the Juntos por el Cambio leader and former president Mauricio Macri from the political caste he denounced for what he regards as their collectivist policies but criticized Juntos por el Cambio member María Eugenia Vidal, who had said that "we share the same values", as governor of the Buenos Aires Province, for not keeping her campaign promises of lower taxes. Milei described Patricia Bullrich, the 2023 Juntos por el Cambio leader, as "part of the Argentine failure".

In a debate before the 2021 primary elections, Frente de Todos candidate Leandro Santoro asked Milei whether he had ever worked for the public sector, since he advocates the state's abolition. Milei had criticized Santoro as "a state parasite" and said: "I understand that you are 45 years old and you have been involved in politics since you were 14. Have you ever worked in the private sector in your life?" Santoro affirmed that Milei was "an employee of the National Congress in 1994 and reported for the former genocidal general Antonio Domingo Bussi", who at the time was a national deputy. In response, Milei acknowledged having worked for Bussi through his Twitter account. In a September 2022 speech to Argentina's Chamber of Deputies, Milei criticized Macri for his proposal not to put a dollar into the Aerolíneas Argentinas, wondering why he did not do that while president, and questioned the government 2023 budget. He also referred to the attempted assassination of Fernández de Kirchner as "not a magnicide [the assassination of a major political figure]", claiming that the term implies that what he regards as the political caste is above the people.

RECAP AND RELEVANCE.

So, why is Javier Milei important for the matter of this book and theory. First of all, he is against Government intervention within a country's economy and says that those that are the best at providing quality education, health, employment, infrastructure development, it is the private sector, the companies that move the country and the economy.

He is pro USD, pro America, meaning will attempt to dollarize Argentinians to end inflation and devaluation problems. Also he is pro Bitcoin given its conditions as wealth creation and preservation instrument, that gives power back to people not to central banks that manipulate. Just as the El Salvador President believes in it too.

The day he got elected all companies listed in the NYSE rallied more than 20% and 30%, same for the estate owned petroleum and gas company YPF increased its price dramatically too.

One week after being elected he is in NY and Washington meeting Biden, Bill Clinton, Wall street bankers and FMI officials.

THE UAE CARBON CREDITS DEAL AHEAD COP 28

We as a family are involved into environmental business, related to conservation projects REDD+ in Colombia that capture Co_2 and GHG, protecting Biodiversity and also contributing to the United Nations SDG's. Sustainable Development Goals that support overall local indigenous communities, their environment, way of living, making their lives better every day.

The Certified Carbon Credits that the forest produces every day are placed into the compliance market or the international voluntary market. You can do this within a platform or brokerage company. In this case we were approached by people in UAE, Dubai. Stating that had contacts to the highest level knowing and working to create one of the largest exchanges in the middle east. Just the same way they have created the largest Crypto exchange and related updated regulations.

In this case our buyers need to have the credits in their power within the registry, so that later they can cancel the carbon credits, Co_2 units, on behalf of the UAE government companies that pollute or to the exchange directly. Own by the government either way.

There is always some person in the middle that a commission has to be paid. USD x per Co_2 ton. This person in Dubai and ourselves in Colombia. When working on the draft brokerage agreement with this person, the subject of a withholding tax in Colombia came to the attention. We started discussing around the matter myself trying to explain the 20% deduction on the invoice to be paid abroad. This became an issue with the counterparty, he saying we wanted to skim him, reduce payment, etc. due to he didn't have to pay any taxes in Dubai why would he do it in Colombia. I said: If you generate income in Colombia, even as a foreigner, there are taxes to be paid. This is the law and we cannot go around it. In any case, we managed to pass the issue and get into a common agreement on the total to be paid (USD) related to the sale of the VCC's to this new customer of ours.

A week later our customer found that these registries or exchanges had relations or companies formed in the USA then, everything came to a halt and didn't want to continue with the transaction to buy carbon credits from us, because they were afraid that the information on the contracts, amount, etc will be shared with USA agencies, causing some kind of sanctions or tax claims.

In the end they said to us, we don't want anything to do with USA, this is why we live in Dubai.

TAX ON JUNK AND ULTRAPROCESSED FOOD

Also called the healthy tax. Recently there has been a new tax approved in Colombia including all kinds of sugar beverages, natural juices or sodas, fast food and snacks with high content on saturated fat, desserts, chocolate, cereals, ice cream, yogurt, ready to eat frozen dishes, ketchup and similar, jam and sausages. It is 10% tax that will increase prices to regular store sellers and consumers.

The government claims this is to bring consciousness to people and their eating habits, but this is not the way, given that most of this products are consumed on a daily basis by most of low income working class people. Basically they just want to raise more money making people believe it is for their health, but on the contrary it is just taking another shot a mental health. Why not to educate the general public on healthy diets, sports practice and the risks of gaining weight.

This pushes inflation higher to some degree, interest rates up, deaccelerate the economy, loss of jobs and devaluation.

It has certainly made people anger to the point they have been writing to the president of our country, on social media with all kinds of insults.

If it is true that they, the government wants the best for our children and young ones, why don't they just eliminate taxes on milk, eggs, bread, rice, and meat, given that there is a large part of the population that just don't have the means to buy these basic products to feed their family.

WHAT ABOUT THE MOON AND SPACE EXPLORATION IMPLICATIONS?

Think few years from now that nations have some more experience in space exploration, all the things we would be able to do and build. All the natural resources that we as humans could take or use to produce whatever the needs, potentially easing environmental pressures on Earth, just like in early times of human civilization, but with a lot more knowledge from our side or starting point. Most likely all minerals will have same or similar composition as in earth, given it all comes from the big bang or same explosion, assuming a valid theory.

Sending people to the Moon, Mars, and to new International Space Stations has significant implications for humanity and the Earth. These missions represent milestones in space exploration and offer a range of benefits, challenges, and potential impacts:

Benefits:

1. **Scientific Discovery:** Missions to the Moon, Mars, and the ISS advance our understanding of space, celestial bodies, and the fundamental processes that govern the universe. They contribute to scientific knowledge in areas like geology, biology, astronomy, and physics.

2. **Technological Advancement:** Space missions drive the development of cutting-edge technologies with applications on Earth. Innovations in areas such as robotics, materials science, communications, and life support systems have practical benefits for various industries and everyday life.

3. **International Collaboration:** Space exploration often involves international cooperation, fostering diplomatic relations and promoting peaceful collaboration among nations.

4. **Inspiration:** Human space exploration inspires the public, especially young people, to pursue careers in science, technology, engineering,

and mathematics (STEM). It encourages curiosity, innovation, and the pursuit of knowledge.

5. **Resource Exploration:** Missions to the Moon and Mars may explore the potential availability of valuable resources, such as water ice, minerals, that could support future lunar or Martian colonies and reduce the burden on Earth's resources.

Challenges:

1. **Cost:** Space exploration missions are expensive, and their funding competes with other societal priorities. Balancing the costs with potential benefits is a constant challenge.

2. **Environmental Impact:** Launching and sustaining missions can have environmental impacts, including rocket emissions, space debris, and the potential contamination of celestial bodies.

3. **Human Health:** Extended space travel poses health risks to astronauts, including exposure to radiation, muscle and bone loss, and psychological challenges due to isolation and confinement.

4. **Space Debris:** The increasing number of objects in Earth's orbit poses a risk of collisions and space debris proliferation, which can endanger both space missions and existing satellites.

5. **Ethical and Legal Issues:** Space exploration raises ethical and legal questions regarding property rights on celestial bodies, planetary protection, and the responsible use of space.

6. **Geopolitical Tensions:** Competition over space resources and strategic positioning could lead to geopolitical tensions.

If we expand our horizons few years from now, many things could be accomplished, like for example no restriction on humans count, as we will have access to many more resources if not infinite looking at the space and ts vastness. Within 10, 20 years we will be able to go into space any time, stay as long as you want, live there and come back whenever you like.

What will be the currency used in space? USD, EUR, CNY, BTC or any other digital medium accepted with interchangeable intrinsic value. An interstellar currency backed by just our purposes, intentions and believes as human race.

Spacex It is now working on the Star Ship, that will be able to take and bring cargo to the space up to 1000 tons or more at a time, then multiply it by any number of ships coming and going like airplanes nowadays.

TAX EVASION PERSONALITIES

12. Nicholas Cage.

The actor only had to pay back $666,000 (plus unspecified interest) of the $3.3 million he owed back in 2008.

11. Wesley Snipes.

The actor was sentenced to 3 years in a Pennsylvania federal prison in 2010.

10. Mike "The Situation" Sorrentino.

The reality star was sentenced to 8 months in prison in 2018.

9. Fat Joe.

The rapper was sentenced to 4 months in prison, a $15,000 fine and one year of supervised release in 2013.

8. Lauryn Hill.

In 2013, the singer was sentenced to a three-month prison sentence after failing to pay around $1.8 million in taxes from 2005 to 2007.

7. Stephen Baldwin.

The actor pled guilty in 2013 & dodged jail time.

He paid the debt off within one year, which allowed him to avoid probation.

6. Ja Rule.

In 2011, the rapper was sentenced to 28 months in prison and agreed to pay $1.1 million in back taxes.

5. Willie Nelson.

In 1991, The country singer owed $6 million to the IRS & released an album called "The IRS Tapes: Who'll Buy My Memories?" of which the IRS reaped much of the profit, totalling $3.6 million.

4. Martha Stewart.

The businesswoman has had her fair share of legal troubles…

Although she was imprisoned for insider trading, she was also required to pay back in full $220,000 to the state of New York due to evading taxes.

3. Marc Anthony.

The singer failed to pay the tax man more than once.

He had to pay back his unpaid taxes totalling $2.5 million in 2007 & $3.4 million in 2010.

Source: Posted on X by Tyler S. Clark ⁂

@DreamFirms

2. Alphonse Gabriel Capone, more commonly known as Al Capone, was an American gangster and one of the most infamous figures of organized crime during the Prohibition era. Here are some key points about Al Capone:

Al Capone was born on January 17, 1899, in Brooklyn, New York, to Italian immigrant parents. He grew up in a tough neighborhood and got involved in criminal activities at a young age.

During the Prohibition era (1920-1933), when the sale of alcoholic beverages was prohibited in the United States, Capone rose to power as a gangster. He became the leader of the Chicago Outfit, a powerful criminal organization.

Bootlegging and Speakeasies:

Capone's criminal activities primarily revolved around bootlegging (illegal alcohol production and distribution) and the operation of speakeasies (underground bars). He profited immensely from the illegal alcohol trade during Prohibition.

Capone was known for his brutal tactics, including the famous St. Valentine's Day Massacre in 1929, in which seven rival gang members were killed. His criminal empire extended into gambling, prostitution, and other illegal activities.

Tax Evasion Conviction:

In 1931, Capone was convicted of tax evasion and sentenced to 11 years in federal prison. He was imprisoned at the Alcatraz Federal Penitentiary on Alcatraz Island, earning him the nickname "Scarface."

1. **Former President Donald Trump** and taxes, several key points and controversies come to mind:

Tax Returns and Transparency:

Donald Trump's tax returns became a subject of significant controversy during his 2016 presidential campaign and throughout his presidency. Unlike most recent presidential candidates, he did not release his tax returns. This lack of transparency raised questions about his finances, potential conflicts of interest, and compliance with tax laws.

The New York Times Investigation:

In September 2020, The New York Times published a series of articles based on a comprehensive investigation of Donald Trump's tax records. The reports alleged that he paid minimal federal income taxes in many years and carried substantial debts. The investigation also raised questions about potential tax avoidance strategies and business losses claimed to reduce tax liability.

Tax Cuts and Jobs Act:

One of the major policy achievements during Trump's presidency was the Tax Cuts and Jobs Act (TCJA) of 2017. The TCJA reduced corporate tax rates, lowered individual income tax rates, and made significant changes to the U.S. tax code. It was the most significant overhaul of the tax system in decades.

Corporate Tax Cuts:

The TCJA reduced the corporate income tax rate from 35% to 21%. Proponents argued that this would make the U.S. more competitive globally and stimulate economic growth. Critics raised concerns about the impact on the federal deficit and income inequality.

Personal Tax Cuts:

The TCJA also cut personal income tax rates, increased the standard deduction, and eliminated some deductions. These changes benefited some taxpayers but were criticized for disproportionately benefiting high-income individuals and corporations.

Impact on the Deficit:

The TCJA was projected to increase the federal budget deficit significantly over the coming years. Some economists argued that the economic growth resulting from the tax cuts would offset these deficits, while others remained skeptical.

Ongoing Legal and Financial Investigations:

Even after leaving the presidency, Donald Trump has been the subject of multiple legal and financial investigations. These include investigations into his business practices, tax returns, and potential tax-related matters by various authorities, including state and local prosecutors.

It's important to note that discussions about Donald Trump's taxes and tax policies remain a topic of political debate and investigation. Opinions on his fiscal and tax-related decisions are often divided along partisan lines, and the full impact of his tax policies, particularly the TCJA, continues to be analyzed and debated.

CONCLUSIONS

All countries have their own problems, issues, challenges, etc. so to come up with one magical solution for all might be kind of difficult to understand by many and also to implement. What we are trying to do with this book or global idea it is to bring awareness to the general audience, politicians and rulers on what can be done in the future to make things better for people and countries.

The basics here or starting point it is that the world it is globalized and after the Covid19 pandemic everything has become more digital, borderless, decentralized and online. Alongside comes Artificial Intelligence that it is developing at a great pace every day. This includes robotics and space exploration industry.

This is why we have seen so much increasing interest in Bitcoin all over the world and also within the regulated financial industry like USA, UK, Hong Kong and Dubai. People tired of the middle man, intermediaries and also central parties trying to control information, deals, assets, transactions, investments, etc. In an effort to get a cut or percentage of the action to themselves.

The Cryptographic industry which it is growing at a huge pace, has around 2 trillion USD in market cap, with many projects and companies inside. One sector called DeFi - decentralized Finance, seems like the future of finance around the globe web3 based. Normally there is a token for transactions or voting, this was minted previously in x quantity, then people start to fund it or invest into it as adoption and real world use grows.

We believe like president Milei from Argentina he is a libertarian and he is against Government intervention within a country's economy. Private efficient companies are the ones ideal at producing and generating wealth. The government it is there to regulate only and help all our citizens to grow and have a better life.

Countries do not belong alone to politicians or governments; they belong to all of its citizens and are composed by its natural resources, infrastructure, industries, companies stablished, people's education and culture, products and services created-offered, sold locally and exported. In the end all of this it is represented by a currency and its strength whatever the name.

The main concern or problem with governments printing or issuing new more currency it is that has to be put as public debt, which in time it comes with an interest rate and there is debt service to be paid for years and years to come. This becomes an infinite loop or spiral which has to be kicked down the road all the time because there will never be enough taxes or public revenue to cover these interest payments. Then again you have another problem called the debt ceiling, which politicians have to come together every year just to forcefully raise it, otherwise there will be a shut down and no payments for public functioning.

Why would you pay interests to people, banks or corporations on something that it is meant for themselves and their benefits either way, only to come back later and charge everybody taxes in an effort to compensate the structural imbalance or deficiency. This only creates a bubble, puts restrictions on public budgets and pressure into countries inflation.

Why is it that United States has managed to grow so much over the last 100 years and maintain their world dominance status or powerhouse? First it is due to their people and immigrants from all over the world as workforce. Second, their vast land and natural resources. Third, they have been printing USD like crazy just to give it back to people, help corporations, private companies grow and to fund all of their development programs in every aspect or sector. The only issue is that they have called it debt which it is not sustainable anymore and will lead to a huge crisis at some point in time.

They even have USD to throw at some other nations with troubles and to finance wars that do not concern them directly. Whether this is ok or not, mismanaged or miss use of funds it's a complete different story now.

We need to rethink our macroeconomic system, how to make it more efficient, sound and sustainable for the long term. This is not about who controls the most money or who owns the most assets, it is about knowing that we are in the same boat and all working together will come ahead in difficult times. It is not about Socialism or Communism, it is about a free market, free economy in which many more opportunities are generated for everyday people providing the right mindset with education, innovation, creativity, positive economic landscape, adequate regulations and that we work towards a promising future for all.

We will be watching how the world economy develops alongside with technology and the new globe reserve currency..

ABOUT THE AUTHOR

Born in Cartago, Colombia in 1981. With studies in Business Administration from the EAN University in Bogota. Also MBA from Universidad Francisco de Vitoria in Madrid, Spain and several other specializations in University of San Francisco, Chicago University and Switzerland on Corporate Finance, Financial Markets, Wealth Management and Project Management.

Most of his life has worked with various companies from the private sector within the commodities trading, mining and construction industries, serving as CFO, CEO and Board of Directors member.

General Manager and founder of Global Investments Corp, an online market place, trading and investments platform.

Entrepreneur, enthusiast about the future of humanity and technology.

www.ingramcontent.com/pod-product-compliance
Lightning Source LLC
Chambersburg PA
CBHW052210220526
45471CB00004B/1899